# Astrology for Beginners

A Guide to Star Signs, Birth Charts, and Personal Growth for Love, Success, Well-Being, and Life Mastery

**Janice AmberLee**

# Table of Contents

# The Cosmic Compass

*People always come into your life for a reason, a season and a lifetime. When you figure out which it is, you know exactly what to do.* —Brian A. "Drew" Chalker

It was a chilly evening when I first met Mrs. Hilda, the eccentric old lady who lived at the end of my street. She had a reputation for being somewhat of an oracle in our neighborhood, always dispensing advice that seemed to be just right for whoever needed it. Some called her a witch, while others said she was simply wise beyond her years.

One day, feeling lost and directionless, I decided to pay her a visit. As I walked into her quaint little cottage, the smell of lavender and old books filled my nostrils. She welcomed me with a warm smile and gestured towards an antique armchair by the fireplace. We talked about life broadly, but more specifically my struggles with finding purpose, understanding myself better, and taking control of my life's narrative. She listened patiently as I poured out my worries about career choices, love life problems, and emotional turmoil; everything that weighed heavily on my heart.

After what felt like hours, she rose from her chair and moved towards an old wooden chest in the corner of the room. From it she retrieved what looked like an ancient map covered in symbols and drawings I didn't understand.

"This," she began, "is your cosmic compass."

She explained how each symbol represented different celestial bodies such as planets and stars, which were all interconnected in ways we could barely fathom. This map was not just any ordinary map; it was a snapshot of where these celestial bodies were positioned at the exact moment of my birth.

Mrs. Hilda told me how astrology could help guide me through life's challenges by providing insights into personality traits linked to zodiac signs or predicting possible future events based on planetary movements.

Mrs. Hilda helped me understand how astrology could serve as a tool for self-discovery, helping me identify strengths I never knew existed within me or weaknesses that held me back from achieving success.

In one instance when I was contemplating a career change, she pointed out how my sun sign, Sagittarius, indicated an inherent love for freedom and exploration. This insight helped me understand why I felt stifled in my desk job and gave me the courage to pursue a more adventurous career path.

Similarly, when I was struggling with understanding my emotions, she explained how my moon sign (representing our emotional side) was in Cancer, which meant that I was naturally sensitive and empathetic. It wasn't a weakness but rather a strength that allowed me to connect deeply with others.

Mrs. Hilda's teachings did not just help me navigate life's ups and downs; they also empowered me to take control of my destiny. By understanding these cosmic influences, I could align myself better with the universe's rhythms, attracting success, love, happiness, or whatever else I desired.

As we concluded our session for that day, I felt like I'd been given a compass to navigate through life's storms. Mrs. Hilda handed me a book that a good friend of hers had written called *Astrology for Beginners*. We agreed to meet regularly so she could help guide me on this new path of self-discovery through astrology. As I left, she gave me one final piece of advice, "Remember," she said with her signature warm smile, "the stars can guide you, but it is you who must walk the path."

# Introduction

Many of us turn to the page of a newspaper, magazine, or online site to check our horoscope and what it says we can expect over the next day, week, month, or year. Although based very loosely on astrological sun signs, there is a lot more to astrology than your horoscope. There are others factors to take into consideration. Your birth chart takes multiple heavenly events into consideration when providing an accurate reading, and because our solar system is constantly on the move, your birth chart is unlikely to be the same as anyone else's, even if you were born on the same date.

There are multiple types of astrology, but this book will focus mainly on modern astrology. Other than sun (zodiac) signs, we'll discuss birth charts and how these can assist you. The most common questions posed to astrologers usually have to do with relationships, finances, and career.

Understanding a little more about yourself through astrology can help you with these and other questions such as dealing with health issues, decision-making, stress relief, attracting positivity, and abundance. By understanding your celestial blueprint—your sun sign traits or moon sign emotions—you can gain insights into your personality or forecast potential future trends.

However, while astrology may provide guidance like a cosmic compass, remember it is ultimately up to us to steer our own ship towards success and happiness.

## Unlocking the Stars: A Step-By-Step Guide to Mastering Astrology and Creating Your Own Charts

Mrs. Hilda suggests that the best way to read this astrology book is to start at the very beginning, learning the basics about astrology, including your star signs and birth chart. She encourages readers to explore how astrology can lead to self-discovery, assist in decision-making, and provide tools for stress relief, attracting love, and finding happiness. As the book progresses, it covers manifesting success, wealth, and abundance. In the final chapters, a step-by-step guide will teach you how to form your own charts. Mrs. Hilda emphasizes that understanding the fundamentals of astrology is essential before you can create and interpret your own charts with confidence.

## MRS. HILDA'S ASTROLOGY QUIZ TIME!

1. **What is the purpose of astrology, according to Mrs. Hilda?**
    a. To forecast future events based on planetary movements.

b. To provide insights into personality traits linked to zodiac signs.

c. A way to gain insight into our personal development and self-discovery.

d. All of the above.

2. **What is the significance of the cosmic compass, as explained by Mrs. Hilda?**

    a. It is a map of celestial bodies at the time of your birth.

    b. It is a tool to predict weather patterns.

    c. It is an ancient artifact with no real meaning.

    d. It is a device used for navigation on sea voyages.

3. **How can astrology serve as a tool for self-discovery, according to Mrs. Hilda's teachings?**

    a. By predicting lottery numbers.

    b. By helping identify strengths and weaknesses within oneself.

    c. By revealing who you will marry in the future.

    d. By providing daily horoscope readings.

4. **In astrology, what does your moon sign represent?**

    a. The career path you should follow.

    b. The number of children in your future.

    c. Our emotional self and how we instinctively respond emotionally.

    d. The city where you will find your true love.

5. **How does your sun sign, in this case Sagittarius, influence you, according to astrology?**

    a. It shows an inherent love for freedom and exploration.

    b. It shows that you are naturally sensitive and empathetic.

    c. It predicts your future career choices.

    d. None of the above.

6. **What was Mrs. Hilda's final piece of advice about astrology?**

    a. "The stars can guide you, but it is you who must walk the path."

    b. "Astrology can solve all your problems."

    c. "You should always consult an astrologer before making any decision."

    d. "Your destiny has been written in the heavens."

7. **What does our moon sign represent?**

    a. Our emotional being.

    b. Our physical strength.

    c. Our intellectual capabilities.

    d. Our spiritual journey.

8. **Who among these groups is turning to astrology for personal growth, according to research by Jeffery (2023)?**

    a. Celebrities.

    b. Millennials and Gen Z.

    c. Middle-aged adults.

d. None of the above.

## *Answers*

1. d. All of the above.
2. a. It is a map of celestial bodies at the time of your birth.
3. b. By helping identify strengths and weaknesses within oneself.
4. c. Our emotional self and how we instinctively respond emotionally
5. a. It shows an inherent love for freedom and exploration.
6. a. "The stars can guide you, but it is you who must walk the path."
7. a. Our emotional being.
8. b. Millennials and Gen Z.

## Chapter 1:

# Astrology 101: The Basics

Not everyone is aware that zodiac signs are depicted through constellations of stars or that other celestial bodies affect personalities, events, and moods. The chances are that, as someone wanting to explore astrology, you already know a little about your sun sign and perhaps about the element you fall under.

## What Is Astrology?

We understand through science that the moon impacts bodies of water on Earth and that without a sun, we wouldn't exist. While these are celestial bodies that have an obvious effect on us and our planet, there are others that play a role too.

Celestial bodies refer to planets, stars, asteroids, minor planets, the moon and its nodes, as well as temporary events such as eclipses and comets passing through our solar system. Astrology looks at these and where they appear in relation to other bodies. This practice helps the astrologer interpret events that may occur as a result of where celestial bodies are at a specific time.

### *Origins of Astrology*

According to Waxman (2018), while no one is certain exactly when astrology was formed, there are indications that it was used in Mesopotamia (now Iraq) almost 3000 years ago to track the position of their gods. Dividing the skies into 12 equal parts, they gave each a name.

The Egyptians were responsible for the idea of constellations and the sun's movement. It is believed that when Alexander the Great liberated Egypt around 2300 years ago, the basis of astrology was formed.

It was then introduced to the Greeks who came up with the 12 zodiac sign names we are familiar with in Western astrology. The Spring Equinox (20 or 21 March) marks the arrival of the beginning of the astrological new year, and as the sun is in Aries at that time of year, it became the first sign of the zodiac.

## *Different Types of Astrology*

There are several types of astrological concepts with some dating back even further than Western Astrology, and some with very specific functions.

### *Modern*

Modern astrology is basically what we know today and makes use of all nine planets. Astrology in its so-called modern form focuses on how the movement of celestial bodies affects us from an inner perspective. In other words, other than the characteristics we are born with according to our birth chart, we may be influenced emotionally or psychologically by the position or phase of the moon and other celestial bodies.

### *Traditional*

Traditional or Western astrology uses seven planets instead of nine. It does not recognize the outer planets (Uranus, Neptune, or Pluto) as having influence on our lives. Each of the seven planets were allocated a day. For instance, Mars is allocated to Tuesday, the Latin word being *Martis.* Traditional astrology also views the houses and planets slightly differently and look at the effects they have on the outer life. It lost popularity in the early 19th century due to its seemingly negative view on human nature.

### *Vedic*

Mention of astrology is found in the Rig Veda, the oldest holy book used in Hinduism which dates back some 3500 years ago. The Rig Veda details the influence different celestial bodies have on us. One's karma is thought to be linked to the position of the planets at the time of birth. Also known as *Jyotish*, Vedic astrology is believed to guide one in their life's journey.

### *Chinese*

The Chinese astrological calendar is determined per year rather than on a monthly basis. At the beginning of each Chinese lunar year (the second new moon after the winter solstice), a new zodiac sign reigns until the following year. The signs are based on animals, and it is said that man displays the attributes of the ruling animal at the time of his birth.

### *Mayan*

While the Mayans were great astronomers and used celestial bodies to plan their planting and harvesting periods, the have a rather complicated astrological system that dates back approximately 2500 years. A sign is determined by the calendar rather than by the stars. To determine a person's character, the combined sun sign, day sign, and 1 of 13 galactic numbers is considered.

The above is a very brief overview of a few types of astrology. There are more such as:

- Mundane analyzes world events and societal changes by examining the movement of slow outer planets like Saturn and Pluto and occurrences of comets and eclipses. These astrologers often predict periods of unrest, wars, or cultural shifts.

- Electional determines the best time for a new undertaking. This can refer to wedding dates, business ventures, career changes, medical procedures, and more.

- Relationship astrology examines the birth charts of two individuals for compatibility, challenges they may face, and the strengths they have as a couple. It's viewed as a third chart with unique characteristics that each partner brings to it.

## *Astrological Ages*

As man evolved, significant shifts occurred approximately every 2100 years when the sun was in a specific sign during a vernal equinox. These marked cultural shifts, changes in thought patterns, and technological evolution and are referred to as *ages*. We'll examine four of them with the approximate dates.

- The Age of Leo, (10,000 to 8,000 BCE), is thought to be the point at which we began to see ourselves as unique individuals. Social hierarchies and priest-kings and rulers emerged. Leaders were seen as divine or semi-divine figures with a direct connection to the divine. Sun worship was significant during this time, with the sun symbolizing life, power, and divine authority. It became an age of artistic and spiritual connection.

- The Age of Cancer (8,740 BC to 6,580 BC) is marked by the worship of the moon and the rise of matriarchal societies. Moon Goddesses became central to spirituality, reflecting the reverence for the divine feminine. Communities were formed and agriculture was implemented, which was representative of nurturing, structure, and growth.

- The Age of Pisces (100 BC to present) is characterized by the rise of dogmatic religions such as Judaism, Christianity, and Islam. These dominated spiritual beliefs and focused on control and guilt and discouraged the connection to nature and spiritual wisdom.

- The Age of Aquarius is believed to be moving in as Pisces moves out of transit. Some believe that we are at the beginning of this age, while others think it is a few hundred years away. The age of Aquarius marks a collective call to reconnect with true inner wisdom. It emphasizes individuality, scientific breakthroughs, and spiritual awakening, encouraging people to seek guidance from within.

## *Astrological Generations*

Astrological generations are determined by the outer planets, particularly by Pluto. Pluto takes around 248 years to circle the sun and travels through each sign to do so. Pluto returns to a sign only every 200 years or so and stays there for 12 to 30 years. Because of this, it is associated with specific generations and the societal changes or traits that show up during those years.

1. Pluto in Cancer (1913-1939) saw the rise of the Silent Generation.

2. Pluto in Leo (1937-1958) became the years of the Boomers.

3. Pluto in Virgo (1956-1972) Generation V is known as the Visual Generation and overlaps with the generations on either side. This is possibly due to the introduction of visual media.

4. Pluto in Libra (1971-1984) and Generation X was born.

5. Pluto in Scorpio (1983-1995) became what we call the Millennial Generation.

6. Pluto in Sagittarius (1995-2008) and the rise of Generation Zoomers (Z).

7. Pluto in Capricorn (2008-2024) sees the birth of Generation Alpha.

8. Pluto in Aquarius (2024-2044) Generation Beta.

## *Galactic Center*

In astrology, the Galactic Center refers to the supermassive black hole at the center of the Milky Way, located around 26-27 degrees in Sagittarius. It serves as a potent source of cosmic energy, impacting personal development, spiritual growth, and higher consciousness. This celestial region embodies themes of truth, freedom, and transformation, making it significant for those seeking deeper understanding and enlightenment in their lives.

Astrologically, alignments with the Galactic Center are thought to reveal profound subconscious insights, encouraging us to shed emotional burdens and embrace a new way of living. This cosmic point acts as a gateway to divine consciousness, providing pathways for spiritual growth and personal transformation, especially in areas reflected in one's natal chart.

## *Ephemeris*

An ephemeris is a tool in astrology that records the positions of celestial bodies—like the sun, moon, planets, and sometimes asteroids—at specific times. It provides detailed tables showing their locations relative to Earth for each day, hour, or minute, typically using zodiac signs and degrees.

Astrologers use an ephemeris to track planetary movements, helping them interpret the effects these positions may have on our birth charts or ongoing planetary transits. For example, it can reveal when a planet enters a new zodiac sign or forms aspects (angles) with other planets, guiding predictions and insights into various life events.

The ephemeris is vital for timing significant astrological moments, such as retrogrades, eclipses, or new and full moons, making it a must-have tool for constructing and interpreting astrological charts.

## Introduction to the 12 Star Signs

In America, 95% of people know what their sun sign is (Accesswire, 2024) and only about 67% know what their blood type is (Lee, 2022). In Britain, 98% know their sun signs (Campion, 2017), and it is estimated that less than half know their blood types (Jenkins, 2018).

The 12 astrological star signs each symbolize distinct personality traits and characteristics, tied to specific dates throughout the year.

1. **Aries (Mar 21 - Apr 19)**: Bold and assertive, Aries are natural leaders with energetic, courageous personalities. They often act impulsively but are enthusiastic and passionate.

2. **Taurus (Apr 20 - May 20)**: People born under this sign are reliable and patient, with a love for comfort and stability. They can be stubborn but are incredibly loyal and dependable.

3. **Gemini (May 21 - Jun 20)**: Known for their adaptability and curiosity, Geminis are excellent communicators. However, they can be indecisive and inconsistent due to their dual nature.

4. **Cancer (Jun 21 - Jul 22)**: Deeply intuitive and emotional, Cancers prioritize family and home. They can be moody but are nurturing and protective.

5. **Leo (Jul 23 - Aug 22)**: Leos are charismatic and love being in the spotlight. They are confident and creative, but can sometimes be prideful or dramatic.

6. **Virgo (Aug 23 - Sep 22)**: Practical and detail-oriented, Virgos strive for perfection. They can be critical but are also highly dependable and organized.

7. **Libra (Sep 23 - Oct 22)**: Libras seek balance and harmony, often acting as mediators in relationships. They are sociable and diplomatic but may struggle with decision-making.

8. **Scorpio (Oct 23 - Nov 21)**: Intense and passionate, Scorpios are known for their determination and loyalty. They tend to be private and mysterious, often diving deeply into emotions.

9. **Sagittarius (Nov 22 - Dec 21)**: Optimistic and adventurous, Sagittarians love exploring new ideas and experiences. They value freedom but may be too blunt or restless at times.

10. **Capricorn (Dec 22 - Jan 19)**: Hardworking and disciplined, Capricorns are focused on achieving long-term goals. They can come across as serious or rigid, but their dedication is unmatched.

11. **Aquarius (Jan 20 - Feb 18)**: Independent and innovative, Aquarians think outside the box. They value individuality but can sometimes seem detached or aloof.

12. **Pisces (Feb 19 - Mar 20)**: Pisces are empathetic and imaginative, often deeply connected to their emotions and intuition. They may appear dreamy or escapist but are compassionate and artistic.

These signs offer insights into people's strengths and challenges, helping to navigate personal relationships and self-understanding, and each sign is linked to one of the four elements, which also shapes their personalities and interactions

## *Elements and Modalities*

The 12 zodiac signs are divided into four elements: Fire, earth, air, and water. Each element represents a fundamental quality of nature and influences how signs express themselves and interact with the world.

### *Fire Signs (Aries, Leo, Sagittarius)*

- **Traits**: Fire signs are known for their enthusiasm, creativity, and determination. They are bold and action-oriented, often pursuing their goals with great intensity.
- **Influence**: Fire signs thrive in situations that require leadership and excitement. However, they can also be impulsive or quick to anger, as fire can be both warming and destructive.
- **Examples**: Aries initiates action, Leo shines with charisma, and Sagittarius seeks adventure and knowledge.

### *Earth Signs (Taurus, Virgo, Capricorn)*

- **Traits**: Earth signs are grounded and value stability, hard work, and material success. They are focused on tangible results and often work methodically to achieve their goals.
- **Influence**: Earth signs are reliable and grounded in reality, making them excellent planners and organizers. However, they can sometimes be too focused on material concerns or resistant to change.
- **Examples**: Taurus enjoys comfort and security, Virgo excels at organization and detail, and Capricorn is ambitious and disciplined.

### *Air Signs (Gemini, Libra, Aquarius)*

- **Traits**: Air signs are thinkers and idea-driven, often focusing on analysis, communication, and relationships. They are adaptable and enjoy exploring new concepts and social connections.

- **Influence**: Air signs are skilled at seeing the bigger picture and excel in diplomacy and innovation. However, they can be detached or indecisive, as they prefer thinking over feeling.

- **Examples**: Gemini loves learning and conversation, Libra seeks harmony and balance in relationships, and Aquarius is a visionary and humanitarian.

### *Water Signs (Cancer, Scorpio, Pisces)*

- **Traits**: Water signs are deeply connected to their feelings and those of others. They are intuitive, often showing empathy and compassion. They are imaginative and may retreat into their emotions for reflection.

- **Influence**: Water signs are in tune with their inner selves and have strong intuition. They excel in nurturing relationships but can also be prone to mood swings or over-sensitivity.

- **Examples**: Cancer nurtures and protects, Scorpio dives deep into emotions and transformation, and Pisces is compassionate and dreamy.

Furthermore, there are three modalities attributed to the different signs.

### *Cardinal Modality (Aries, Cancer, Libra, Capricorn)*

Cardinal signs are initiators and leaders. They are action-oriented and energetic, often taking charge to start new projects or ideas. This modality brings dynamism and the drive to set things in motion, but these signs may sometimes struggle with follow-through.

- **Example**: Aries takes bold action, Cancer nurtures new emotional bonds, Libra initiates partnerships, and Capricorn builds long-term plans.

### *Fixed Modality (Taurus, Leo, Scorpio, Aquarius)*

Fixed signs are steady, reliable, determined, and sometimes resistant to change. They provide consistency, stability, and focus on maintaining or developing what has already been started. They are the people who get things done and may be persistent. However, negative traits may show up as being inflexible or stubborn.

This may reflect in each sign a little differently:

- Taurus secures resources.
- Leo exudes confidence.
- Scorpio deepens commitments.
- Aquarius holds firm to its ideals.

### *Mutable Modality (Gemini, Virgo, Sagittarius, Pisces)*

- **Traits**: Mutable signs are adaptable, flexible, and open to change. They are the "finishers" of the zodiac, bringing things to completion by adjusting to circumstances. However, their adaptability can sometimes lead to indecision or inconsistency.
- **Summary**: Mutable signs bring closure and adapt to shifts in energy, offering flexibility.
- **Example**: Gemini adapts through communication, Virgo through detail, Sagittarius through exploration, and Pisces through empathy.

These modalities help explain how each sign operates within the broader astrological framework, revealing how they start, maintain, or adjust to different aspects of life.

## Progression Quiz

1. **What is the definition of *astrology*?**
    a. The study of celestial bodies and their impact on human lives.
    b. The study of stars and galaxies.
    c. The study of planets and their moons.
    d. The science that deals with the origin, structure, and space-time relationships of the universe.
2. **Where did astrology originate from?**
    a. Ancient Rome
    b. Medieval Europe
    c. Ancient Greece
    d. Ancient Babylon
3. **What are the four elements in astrology?**
    a. Fire, water, earth, air
    b. Water, fire, metal, wood
    c. Earth, wind, fire, water
    d. Air, earth, metal, wood

4. **Which one is not a modality in astrology?**

    a. Cardinal

    b. Fixed

    c. Mutable

    d. Flexible

5. **What does an ephemeris provide information about?**

    a. The position of celestial bodies at any given time.

    b. The characteristics associated with each star sign.

    c. The age of the universe according to astrological calculations.

    d. Detailed horoscope predictions for people.

## *Answers*

1. a. The study of celestial bodies and their impact on human lives.
2. d. Ancient Babylon
3. a. Fire, water, earth, air
4. d. Flexible
5. a. The position of celestial bodies at any given time.

Chapter 2:

# Star Signs: Your Core Identity

Your star sign, also called a *sun sign* or *zodiac sign*, plays a key role in your character. However, understanding who you are requires the knowledge of more than just your star sign. There are other factors and elements, such as decans, steroids, ascendant signs, and the moon, that come into play and influence you. Knowing how these elements work explains why two people born in the same sign may have differences unique to each.

## The Role of Your Sun Sign

Sun signs in astrology represent our core identity, revealing key aspects of who we are at a fundamental level. The sun symbolizes the essence of our character, embodying our personality, self-expression, and life purpose. It reflects our central traits; how we approach life, what motivates us, and how we interact with the world around us.

Our sun sign also highlights our ego and vitality, shaping how we project ourselves outwardly. It governs our ambitions, personal desires, and how we seek recognition. While the moon and rising signs influence our emotions and social interactions, the sun sign is like our inner compass, guiding our sense of self and purpose throughout life.

## The 12 Star Signs

Each zodiac sign is associated with a constellation of stars. These are depicted as symbols and attributed to each sign. They are further assigned ruling planets, metals, colors, plants, and more. For ease of reference each is listed beneath the associated signs.

### *Aries (March 21 - April 19)*

Aries is associated with the Ram, a figure that brings to mind charging forward and being somewhat temperamental. The planet Mars and the element of fire give this sign drive and determination.

#### *Associations*

- Element: Fire
- Modality: Cardinal
- Ruling Planet: Mars

- Symbol: The Ram
- Opposite Sign: Libra
- Keyword: Action
- Phrase: "I am"
- Aspiration: To lead and conquer new challenges
- Color: Red
- Metal: Iron
- Crystals: Carnelian, Bloodstone, Ruby
- Body: Head, brain, eyes
- Vulnerabilities: Headaches, migraines, sinus issues
- Plants: Thistle, honeysuckle
- Herbs: Basil, cayenne pepper, ginger

### *Characteristics*

- Energetic, bold, and assertive
- Independent and pioneering
- Direct and honest, sometimes blunt

### *Strengths*

- Natural leaders with high confidence
- Passionate and driven in pursuits

- Quick decision-makers and action-takers

*Challenges*

- Impulsive and impatient
- Struggles with authority or rules
- Can be overly competitive and self-centered

## *Taurus (April 20 - May 20)*

Taurus is associated with the bull, the epitome of patience, and being methodical. The planet Venus symbolizes love and the enjoyment of all that is beautiful. The Earth, as its designated planet, gives Taurus stability but also a tendency to dig their heels in.

*Associations*

- Element: Earth

- Modality: Fixed
- Ruling Planet: Venus
- Symbol: The Bull
- Opposite Sign: Scorpio
- Keyword: Stability
- Phrase: "I have"
- Aspiration: To achieve security and enjoy life's pleasures
- Color: Green, pink
- Metal: Copper
- Crystals: Emerald, Rose Quartz, Jade
- Body: Neck, throat, thyroid
- Vulnerabilities: Sore throats, neck stiffness
- Plants: Apple, cypress, rose
- Herbs: Mint, thyme, valerian

### *Characteristics*

- Loyal, practical, and grounded
- Values stability and security
- Appreciates beauty, comfort, and luxury

*Strengths*

- Determined, patient, and reliable
- Good with managing finances and material resources
- Strong sense of loyalty and commitment

*Challenges*

- Can be stubborn and resistant to change
- Overly materialistic or indulgent
- Tendency to hold grudges or be possessive

## *Gemini (May 21 - June 20)*

*Associations*

- Element: Air

- Modality: Mutable
- Ruling Planet: Mercury
- Symbol: The Twins
- Opposite Sign: Sagittarius
- Keyword: Communication
- Phrase: "I think"
- Aspiration: To learn and share knowledge
- Color: Yellow
- Metal: Mercury
- Crystals: Citrine, Agate, Tiger's Eye
- Body: Arms, lungs, nervous system
- Vulnerabilities: Respiratory issues, anxiety
- Plants: Lavender, fern
- Herbs: Dill, parsley, anise

### *Characteristics*

- Curious, social, and adaptable
- Excellent communicators
- Dual-natured with diverse interests

*Strengths*

- Quick-witted and versatile
- Highly communicative and good at networking
- Can juggle multiple projects at once

*Challenges*

- Prone to inconsistency and indecisiveness
- Easily distracted or scattered
- Struggles with commitment and staying focused

## *Cancer (June 21 - July 22)*

*Associations*

- Element: Water

- Modality: Cardinal
- Ruling Planet: Moon
- Symbol: The Crab
- Opposite Sign: Capricorn
- Keyword: Nurturing
- Phrase: "I feel"
- Aspiration: To create emotional security and protect loved ones
- Color: Silver, white
- Metal: Silver
- Crystals: Moonstone, Pearl, Selenite
- Body: Chest, stomach, breasts
- Vulnerabilities: Digestive issues, chest pains
- Plants: Willow, lotus, water lily
- Herbs: Chamomile, sage, lemon balm

### *Characteristics*

- Nurturing, sensitive, and emotional
- Protective of loved ones and home
- Strong intuitive abilities

### *Strengths*

- Empathetic and compassionate
- Excellent caretakers, both emotionally and physically
- Loyal and protective, especially towards family

### *Challenges*

- Prone to mood swings and emotional overwhelm
- Can be overly protective or clingy
- Struggles with vulnerability and letting go of the past

## *Leo (July 23 - August 22)*

### *Associations*

- Element: Fire

- Modality: Fixed
- Ruling Planet: Sun
- Symbol: The Lion
- Opposite Sign: Leo
- Keyword: Confidence
- Phrase: "I will"
- Aspiration: To express creativity and receive recognition
- Color: Gold, orange
- Metal: Gold
- Crystals: Sunstone, Amber, Topaz
- Body: Heart, spine, upper back
- Vulnerabilities: Heart problems, back pain
- Plants: Sunflower, marigold, citrus trees
- Herbs: Rosemary, cinnamon, saffron

***Characteristics***

- Charismatic, confident, and self-expressive
- Loves being the center of attention
- Generous and warm-hearted

*Strengths*

- Natural leaders with a magnetic personality
- Creative and enthusiastic
- Loyal and protective of loved ones

*Challenges*

- Prone to arrogance or being self-centered
- Needs constant validation and attention
- Can be domineering or inflexible

## *Virgo (August 23 - September 22)*

*Associations*

- Element: Earth

- Modality: Mutable
- Ruling Planet: Mercury
- Symbol: The Virgin
- Opposite Sign: Pisces
- Keyword: Perfection
- Phrase: "I analyze"
- Aspiration: To refine and perfect all aspects of life
- Color: Earth tones, green, brown
- Metal: Mercury
- Crystals: Sapphire, Jasper, Amazonite
- Body: Digestive system, intestines
- Vulnerabilities: Digestive disorders, stress
- Plants: Lavender, ivy
- Herbs: Fennel, sage, rosemary

### *Characteristics*

- Practical, analytical, and detail-oriented
- Organized and hardworking
- Health-conscious and service-oriented

***Strengths***

- Excellent problem-solving skills and attention to detail
- Highly reliable and responsible
- Great at organizing and optimizing tasks

***Challenges***

- Perfectionism and overly critical, both of self and others
- Prone to anxiety or worry
- Struggles with letting go of control

## *Libra (September 23 - October 22)*

***Associations***

- Element: Air

- Modality: Cardinal
- Ruling Planet: Venus
- Symbol: The Scales
- Opposite Sign: Aries
- Keyword: Balance
- Phrase: "I balance"
- Aspiration: To create harmony in relationships and environments
- Color: Pink, light blue
- Metal: Copper
- Crystals: Lapis Lazuli, Opal, Rose Quartz
- Body: Kidneys, lower back
- Vulnerabilities: Kidney issues, lower back pain
- Plants: Roses, violets
- Herbs: Thyme, catnip, licorice

### *Characteristics*

- Charming, diplomatic, and peace-loving
- Values harmony, fairness, and beauty
- Social and relationship-oriented

### *Strengths*

- Excellent mediators and negotiators
- Tactful and considerate
- Strong sense of aesthetics and beauty

### *Challenges*

- Prone to indecisiveness and people-pleasing
- Avoids confrontation at all costs
- Can be superficial or overly focused on appearances

## *Scorpio (October 23 - November 21)*

### *Associations*

- Element: Water

- Modality: Fixed
- Ruling Planet: Pluto and Mars
- Symbol: The Scorpion
- Opposite Sign: Taurus
- Keyword: Transformation
- Phrase: "I desire"
- Aspiration: To understand the depths of life and experience profound change
- Color: Black, maroon
- Metal: Steel
- Crystals: Obsidian, Garnet, Malachite
- Body: Reproductive organs, bowels
- Vulnerabilities: Reproductive system issues, infections
- Plants: Cactus, hemlock
- Herbs: Sage, black cohosh, ginseng

### *Characteristics*

- Intense, passionate, and mysterious
- Highly intuitive and perceptive
- Strong emotional depth

*Strengths*

- Determined and resourceful
- Excellent at uncovering hidden truths
- Loyal and protective of loved ones

*Challenges*

- Prone to jealousy and possessiveness
- Can be secretive or manipulative
- Struggles with trust and forgiveness

## *Sagittarius (November 22 - December 21)*

*Associations*

- Element: Fire

- Modality: Mutable
- Ruling Planet: Jupiter
- Symbol: The Archer
- Opposite Sign: Gemini
- Keyword: Freedom
- Phrase: "I see"
- Aspiration: To explore and understand the meaning of life
- Color: Purple, royal blue
- Metal: Tin
- Crystals: Amethyst, Turquoise, Lapis Lazuli
- Body: Hips, thighs, liver
- Vulnerabilities: Hip pain, liver issues
- Plants: Dandelion, clover
- Herbs: Sage, anise, clove

### *Characteristics*

- Adventurous, optimistic, and free-spirited
- Loves travel, learning, and exploration
- Philosophical and idealistic

*Strengths*

- Enthusiastic and open-minded
- Highly independent and freedom-loving
- Strong sense of humor and positivity

*Challenges*

- Prone to restlessness and impatience
- Can be tactless or overly blunt
- Struggles with commitment and staying grounded

## *Capricorn (December 22 - January 19)*

*Associations*

- Element: Earth

- Modality: Cardinal
- Ruling Planet: Saturn
- Symbol: The Goat
- Opposite Sign: Cancer
- Keyword: Discipline
- Phrase: "I use"
- Aspiration: To achieve long-term goals through hard work
- Color: Black, gray
- Metal: Lead
- Crystals: Onyx, Garnet, Jet
- Body: Knees, bones, teeth
- Vulnerabilities: Arthritis, dental issues
- Plants: Pine, ivy
- Herbs: Comfrey, sage, wintergreen

### *Characteristics*

- Disciplined, ambitious, and responsible
- Hardworking and goal-oriented
- Traditional and values structure

*Strengths*

- Highly disciplined and self-controlled
- Excellent at planning and achieving long-term goals
- Strong sense of responsibility and ethics

*Challenges*

- Can be overly serious or rigid
- Prone to workaholism and burnout
- Struggles with expressing emotions or vulnerability

## *Aquarius (January 20 - February 18)*

*Associations*

- Element: Air

- Modality: Fixed
- Ruling Planet: Uranus and Saturn
- Symbol: The Water Bearer
- Opposite Sign: Leo
- Keyword: Innovation
- Phrase: "I know"
- Aspiration: To revolutionize and uplift society
- Color: Electric blue, turquoise
- Metal: Uranium
- Crystals: Amethyst, Garnet, Sapphire
- Body: Ankles, circulatory system
- Vulnerabilities: Circulatory issues, sprains
- Plants: Orchid, eucalyptus
- Herbs: Frankincense, myrrh, lavender

### *Characteristics*

- Independent, innovative, and forward-thinking
- Values individuality and uniqueness
- Humanitarian and socially conscious

*Strengths*

- Visionary and inventive, often ahead of their time
- Highly intellectual and objective
- Strong sense of social justice and community

*Challenges*

- Can be detached or emotionally distant
- Prone to rebellious or contrarian behavior
- Struggles with intimacy or emotional vulnerability

## *Pisces (February 19 - March 20)*

*Associations*

- Element: Water

- Modality: Mutable
- Ruling Planet: Neptune and Jupiter
- Symbol: Two Fish
- Opposite Sign: Virgo
- Keyword: Intuition
- Phrase: "I believe"
- Aspiration: To transcend the material world and connect with the spiritual
- Color: Sea green, lavender
- Metal: Tin
- Crystals: Aquamarine, Amethyst, Moonstone
- Body: Feet, immune system
- Vulnerabilities: Foot pain, immune disorders
- Plants: Water lily, lotus
- Herbs: Sage, lemon balm, thyme

### *Characteristics*

- Compassionate, intuitive, and artistic
- Highly sensitive and empathetic
- Dreamy and imaginative

### *Strengths*

- Creative and emotionally in tune
- Excellent at empathizing with others
- Strong intuitive and spiritual abilities

### *Challenges*

- Prone to escapism or avoiding reality
- Can be overly sensitive or easily overwhelmed
- Struggles with boundaries and self-discipline

## Opposite Signs

You may have heard the saying the opposites attract. Of course, this is not a hard and fast rule, and there's a lot more to consider in terms of astrology, although generally speaking, your opposite sign is likely the most compatible partnership for you.

In romantic relationships, one partner often possesses a quality the other lacks, creating a complementary dynamic. In friendships, an opposite sign can reveal something intrinsic to you that you may not fully understand or appreciate. This helps you learn more about yourself through their contrasting perspective, offering growth and new insights.

When signs are positioned opposite each other on the zodiac wheel, they share key traits despite their differences. These shared values often create attraction and strong connections even though their differing approaches can lead to tension. Their similarities form the basis for understanding, while their differing perspectives can both complement and challenge the relationship. An example, Taurus and Scorpio both value security, but Taurus focuses on material stability, while Scorpio prioritizes emotional safety.

## *Aries and Libra*

As the boldest of the fire signs, Aries is impulsive, headstrong, and jumps into action with fierce energy. On the other hand, Libra thrives on careful deliberation, weighing options, and seeking harmony. When these two opposite signs connect, whether in love or friendship, the chemistry is immediate. Their contrasting qualities create a dynamic that sparks instant attraction, blending Aries' intensity with Libra's quest for balance.

In friendship, Aries and Libra create a harmonious duo. Aries encourages the more gentle and indecisive Libra to prioritize their own needs and assert themselves when necessary. Conversely, Libra helps Aries slow down and consider various perspectives before diving into action, preventing a one-track mindset. This exchange fosters mutual growth, allowing both signs to learn from each other's strengths and weaknesses.

## *Taurus and Scorpio*

The Taurus-Scorpio relationship is driven by intense passion. Both signs are deeply connected to sensuality, creating an almost magnetic bond. For Taurus, pleasure comes through physical indulgence, whether it's savoring fine food, luxurious textures, or intimacy. Scorpio, however, experiences physical pleasure, especially sex, as a profound and transformative act. While Scorpio may feel emotions deeply, they don't always reveal those feelings, adding a layer of mystery to the connection between these two fixed signs.

In friendship, Taurus and Scorpio form a strong bond through their mutual drive for success and determination. Both appreciate life's luxuries and enjoy indulging in shared experiences. Even without a romantic connection, their love for the finer things brings them together for fun and meaningful moments. Their tenacity and shared values make for a deep and enduring friendship, rooted in their mutual pursuit of achievement and enjoyment of life's pleasures.

### *Gemini and Sagittarius*

Gemini and Sagittarius share a mutual love for exploration, but express it differently. Curious Gemini explores through intellectual, social, and sexual avenues, while Sagittarius prefers adventure through travel and broad experiences. Their biggest challenge lies in commitment, as both crave freedom and need personal space, even in strong relationships. Gemini focuses on details, while Sagittarius is more of a big-picture thinker. To avoid stagnation, they need to maintain shared interests and allow room for individuality, balancing their thirst for excitement with a sense of partnership.

In friendship, Gemini tends to get caught up in details, and Sagittarius can help broaden their perspective by encouraging them to think big. Sagittarius, as a deep thinker, seeks in-depth knowledge, which can inspire Gemini to explore subjects more thoroughly rather than skimming the surface. For Sagittarius, who often forms strong beliefs based on instinct and emotion, Gemini offers guidance in gathering external information to build a more objective, well-rounded perspective.

### *Cancer and Capricorn*

When Cancer and Capricorn come together, they form a powerful, well-balanced partnership. Cancer focuses on creating a nurturing home and craves emotional and financial security, while Capricorn is driven by ambition and goal-setting. Both share a commitment to providing stability for their loved ones, combining Cancer's domestic instincts with Capricorn's professional determination. Their mutual sense of duty and responsibility makes them a dynamic team, blending the best of home and career life to build a secure future together. Both Capricorn and Cancer share a deep sense of loyalty and responsibility, though they express it differently.

Capricorn provides through hard work and achievement, while Cancer nurtures and protects emotionally. Cancer can teach Capricorn to seek internal fulfillment rather than external validation, encouraging self-care. Meanwhile, Capricorn helps Cancer step out of their comfort zone and pursue their goals with more confidence. Together, they balance emotional support and ambition, creating a strong foundation for home and personal growth.

## *Leo and Aquarius*

Leo and Aquarius, both fixed signs, are known for their resilience in relationships, creating bonds that are hard to break. Leo thrives on passion and craves admiration, while Aquarius seeks intellectual engagement and values being accepted for their creativity. Despite their differences—Leo focusing more on self-expression and Aquarius on collective ideals—they both value community and friendships, which strengthens their connection as a couple. Their unique energies complement each other, with Leo shining individually and Aquarius contributing to the greater whole.

Aquarius and Leo make an intriguing pair, whether in friendship or romance. Leo encourages Aquarius to tap into their own creativity, bringing warmth and passion to balance Aquarius' intellectual side. On the flip side, Aquarius helps Leo share their talents with the world and embrace collaboration, while still respecting their mutual need for independence. Both signs value autonomy, but together, they teach each other the importance of balancing self-expression with contributing to a larger community.

## *Virgo and Pisces*

Virgo and Pisces, both mutable signs, bring balance to each other despite their differing outlooks. Virgo's grounded nature complements Pisces' dreamy tendencies, helping turn visions into reality with practical advice and structured plans. Meanwhile, Pisces encourages Virgo to let go of over-analysis and embrace creativity. Their connection ignites mental and emotional passion, as Virgo thrives on learning and Pisces taps into deeper wisdom. Together, they inspire each other, with Virgo providing stability and Pisces nurturing imaginative growth.

While Virgo and Pisces might seem like opposites, both share a passion for helping and healing, though from distinct viewpoints. Virgo approaches life with a perfectionist eye, keen on refining details and organizing the bigger picture. Pisces, on the other hand, brings an idealistic and deeply empathetic perspective, offering compassion to any situation. Virgo helps Pisces break complex issues into manageable parts, preventing overwhelm, while Pisces encourages Virgo to embrace imperfections, teaching them to be more forgiving of flaws, both in themselves and others.

## Decanates

The zodiac is depicted as a circle, or wheel, divided into 12 equal parts. Decans (or decanates) are subdivisions of the zodiac signs that help refine personality traits based on the position or degree of the sun within a specific sign. Each zodiac sign spans 30 degrees, and each sign can be divided into three decans of 10 degrees each.

1. First Decan (0-10 degrees): This is the purest expression of the sign's qualities. People born in this decan typically exhibit the most typical traits associated with that sign.

2. Second Decan (10-20 degrees): The characteristics of this decan blend in qualities from the next sign in the same element (e.g., for Taurus, it would blend with Virgo). This adds a layer of complexity and might modify the primary traits of the sign.

3. Third Decan (20-30 degrees): This decan incorporates influences from the next sign after the second decan. It brings further nuances and might result in unique personality traits that differ from the first decan.

Below is an example of how this might work with the sign Aries.

- First Decan (Aries 0-10 degrees): Pure Aries traits: bold, assertive, and energetic.
- Second Decan (Aries 10-20 degrees): Influenced by Leo, leading to a more dramatic or charismatic Aries.
- Third Decan (Aries 20-30 degrees): Influenced by Sagittarius, adding a philosophical or adventurous flair.

## The Four Angular Points

The four angular points in astrology refer to the ascendant, descendant, midheaven, and Imum Coeli points. These appear on the cusp of different areas within your birth chart.

You'll remember that the zodiac is a wheel that consists of 12 divisions.

1. The ascendant appears on the cusp of the 1st House (the self) of your chart.
2. The descendant appears directly opposite and is on the cusp of the 7th House (relationships) of your chart.
3. The Imum Coeli appears on the cusp of the 4th House (family and home).
4. The midheaven appears on the cusp of the 10th House (work).

### *Ascendants*

This is also referred to as a rising sign. This is the sign that was ascending on the Eastern side of your chart at the time of your birth in the 9 o'clock position. Therefore, it has a certain amount of influence on your behavior and emotional state. Knowing what your rising sign is will help you understand the personality you show the outside world, as well as how you deal with emotional issues. These insights can help with managing relationships, challenges, and personal development.

- Outward Behavior (Persona): The rising sign is like the "mask" you wear in public, the first impression you give to others. It influences your appearance, social behavior, and how you initially interact with the world. While your sun sign represents your core identity, the ascendant shows how you express that identity externally. For example, someone with a Leo sun might have a quiet and modest Virgo rising, making them seem reserved at first.

- Emotional Life (Reactions and Coping): Because the ascendant affects how you navigate challenges, it shapes your instinctual reactions, emotional defenses, and how you handle stress. For example, an Aries sun sign with Cancer rising, may have Cancer influencing a quick and assertive attitude with more sensitivity and empathy than usually displayed by a typical Aries.

- Long-Term Effect: The ascendant and evolves with you as you grow, influencing your life path, how you fulfill your potential, and provides insights as far as emotional growth and adaptability are concerned. For instance, an Aquarius rising may seek independence and unconventional experiences to evolve emotionally, while a Taurus rising seeks stability and security.

## *Descendants*

While your ascendant shapes your instinctive drives and personal style, your descendant reveals your deeper relationship needs.

It often illustrates why opposites attract, which might explain why your partners don't always click with your friend group. Finding someone with traits aligned with your descendant can bring your life a sense of harmony and stability. The descendant is the gateway to your 7th House which deals with relationships. Located at the 3 o'clock position on your chart, it marks the cusp of this house, directly across from your ascendant. Your descendant offers insights into what you need in a committed partnership and the kind of bond that will fulfill you. It goes beyond the excitement of the honeymoon phase, focusing instead on the practical side of long-term relationships such as mutual support, respect, and empathy.

### *Imum Coeli*

The Imum Coeli (IC) marks the cusp of the 4th House in your birth chart. It represents the most intimate aspects of your life, including home, family dynamics, early childhood, and your relationship with nurturing parental figures. The sign governing your IC reveals how you approach personal matters such as the relationships that provide security and your choice of home environment.

The IC also reflects family relations and the type of home you want as an adult. Planets aspecting the IC also influences the way its energy manifests. For example, Neptune's aspect could indicate a challenging childhood, while Mercury's aspect suggests an active, social upbringing.

On a practical level, the IC helps guide your decisions about where to live and how you define a comfortable space. It connects to themes of childhood development, inner security, nurturing, and family, and shares similarities with Cancer.

### *Midheaven*

The midheaven, or Medium Coeli (MC) is often found near the top of the birth chart, and is the most public point in astrology, representing your career path, social standing, and reputation. Although it sits high on the chart wheel, its directional alignment is South.

It represents your most visible accomplishments in society, including the material things you hold value to. The public face you present, contrasting with the more personal image of your ascendant is also a factor of the MC as well as your sense of responsibility and social status.

The MC reflects your higher aspirations, guiding your long-term goals and shaping your professional life. It can also symbolize the parent or authority figure who most influenced your sense of duty, discipline, and societal standing. It could go as far as representing an employer, government, or other figures of authority in your life.

Your MC sign reveals insights into your career, your attitude toward success, and your awareness of societal expectations. Planetary aspects to the MC provide further details, showing the ease or challenges that you may encounter in pursuing your ambitions.

The MC is the starting point of the 10th House in most house systems, revealing your professional life, social role, and sense of achievement.

## Realizing Your Full Potential Based on Your Star Sign

Here are unique tips on how each zodiac sign can unlock its potential based on their characteristics, focusing on strengths and challenges. These suggestions will help you leverage your natural traits to reach your full potential:

### *Aries: Harnessing Energy for Leadership*

- **Strengths**: Determined, ambitious, and fearless.
- **Tip**: To maximize your potential, channel your energy into leadership roles that demand quick decision-making and innovation. To avoid burnout, you need to counter your enthusiastic nature patience.
- **Growth**: Practice mindfulness to temper impulsiveness and avoid conflict, leading to more sustainable success.

### *Taurus: Building on Consistency and Stability*

- **Strengths**: Determined, steadfast, and pragmatic.
- **Tip**: Use your steadfast nature to build long-term goals that align with your values. Connect with nature or engage in tactile activities like gardening to ground yourself.
- **Growth**: Embrace flexibility and adaptability to prevent getting stuck in routines that no longer serve your goals.

### *Gemini: Channeling Curiosity Into Mastery*

- **Strengths**: Flexible, communicative, and intellectually curious.
- **Tip**: Break goals into smaller tasks to keep your focus while still exploring various interests. Public speaking, writing, and intellectual challenges will sharpen your strengths.
- **Growth**: Cultivate patience and depth in learning to avoid spreading yourself too thin.

### *Cancer: Nurturing Others and Yourself*

- **Strengths**: Compassionate, caring, and intuitive.
- **Tip**: Lean into your caregiving nature by setting healthy emotional boundaries. Focus on careers or personal goals that allow you to support others while maintaining self-care practices.
- **Growth**: Protect your energy from negativity and strengthen your psychic and intuitive abilities through mindfulness.

### *Leo: Radiating Confidence and Creativity*

- **Strengths**: Self-assured, innovative, and leading.
- **Tip**: Embrace creative outlets like art or performance to express your vibrant energy. Cultivating leadership skills through workshops or mentorship will elevate your potential.
- **Growth**: Practice humility and share the spotlight to foster teamwork, avoiding ego clashes.

### *Virgo: Embracing Perfection Through Compassion*

- **Strengths**: Precise, pragmatic, and analytical.
- **Tip**: Leverage your analytical nature by setting realistic, achievable goals. Celebrate small wins and delegate tasks to avoid overworking yourself.
- **Growth**: Learn to accept imperfection as part of progress, reducing self-criticism and embracing collaboration.

### *Libra: Harmonizing for Personal and Collective Growth*

- **Strengths**: Courteous, peaceful, and just.
- **Tip**: Use your natural ability to mediate and build strong partnerships. Trust your intuition when making decisions to avoid indecisiveness.
- **Growth**: Practice decisiveness and set clear boundaries to ensure you don't lose momentum while weighing options.

### *Scorpio: Transforming Through Focus and Intensity*

- **Strengths**: Perseverant, ingenious, and emotionally deep.
- **Tip**: Channel your passion into transformative goals. Focus on long-term projects that allow you to use your analytical and investigative talents.
- **Growth**: Learn to let go of control in situations where it isn't needed, and trust others more to avoid burnout.

### *Sagittarius: Expanding Horizons With Optimism*

- **Strengths**: Adventurous, optimistic, and thirsty for knowledge.
- **Tip**: Pursue experiences that broaden your worldview, such as travel or higher education. Use your naturally positive outlook to motivate others.
- **Growth**: Stay grounded by focusing on follow-through, and avoid over-committing to too many ventures at once.

### *Capricorn: Structuring Success Through Discipline*

- **Strengths**: Ambitious, diligent, and practical.
- **Tip**: Build success with strategic, long-term planning. Focus on creating a strong foundation through disciplined routines and hard work.
- **Growth**: Remember to balance work with relaxation, preventing burnout by prioritizing self-care.

### *Aquarius: Innovating Through Collaboration*

- **Strengths**: Inventive, non-conformist, and humanitarian.
- **Tip**: Use your visionary thinking to push the boundaries of innovation. Engage in collaborative projects that allow you to champion causes that matter to you.
- **Growth**: Practice empathy and consider the perspectives of others, especially when your independence leads to detachment.

### *Pisces: Tapping Into Intuition for Fulfillment*

- **Strengths**: Creative, empathetic, and intuitive.
- **Tip**: Use your imagination and compassion in artistic or healing professions. Practices like meditation or journaling can enhance your intuitive abilities.
- **Growth**: Create clear boundaries and stay grounded to avoid being overwhelmed by emotions or unrealistic expectations.

## Progression Quiz

1. **Which of the following is NOT one of the 12 star signs in astrology?**
    a. Capricorn
    b. Scorpio
    c. Ophiuchus
    d. Pisces

2. **What does your sun sign in astrology represent?**

    a. Your emotional nature and instincts.

    b. Your core identity and ego.

    c. Your communication style.

    d. Your future destiny.

3. **What are decanates in astrology?**

    a. They are divisions within each astrological sign that give more detail about a person's character traits.

    b. They are celestial bodies that influence a person's horoscope.

    c. They are periods of time when certain star signs have more influence than others.

    d. They refer to the transition from one zodiac sign to another.

4. **What role does the moon sign play in an astrological profile?**

    a. It determines their career path and ambition?

    b. It represents their love life and relationships with others.

    c. It governs their emotional life, moods, and subconscious self.

    d. It signifies their health and physical constitution.

5. **Which statement is true regarding rising signs (or ascendant) in astrology?**

    a. They indicate a person's past-life karma.

b. They signify a person's hidden talents or skills they may not be aware of yet.

c. They represent how individuals present themselves to the world, first impressions, and physical appearance.

d. All of these statements are correct.

## *Answers*

1. c. Ophiuchus
2. b. Your core identity and ego.
3. a. They are divisions within each astrological sign that give more detail about a person's character traits.
4. c. It governs their emotional life, moods, and subconscious self.
5. c. They represent how individuals present themselves to the world, first impressions, and physical appearance.

Chapter 3:

# Exploring Your Birth Chart

Although star signs give a broad overview of personality, the planets, being closer to Earth, have a stronger and more direct influence on our lives. The planets' positions at our birth and their interactions with our star sign creates a more detailed astrological profile that indicates specific traits, behaviors, and patterns.

## Introduction to the Birth Chart

Each planet governs different aspects of our character, including communication, love, and career choice. Furthermore, asteroids and other celestial bodies provide even more depth, revealing hidden patterns and personal growth opportunities. This interplay between the different celestial bodies forms the foundation of understanding astrological events, predictions, and birth charts.

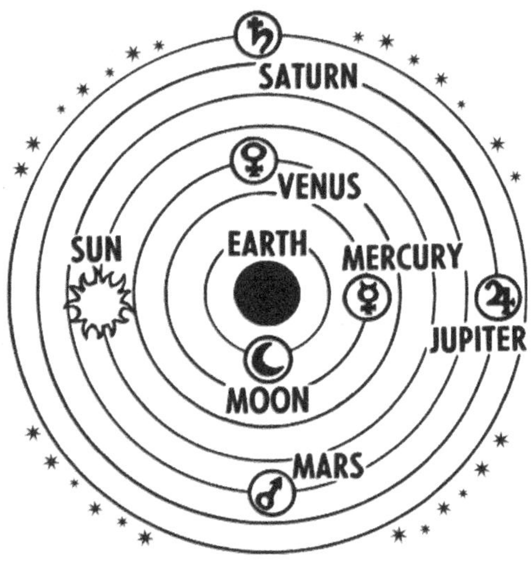

A birth chart is a cosmic snapshot of the exact moment you were born. It reflects the precise positions of the planets and which zodiac constellations they occupied. Each chart differs, with some charts showing several planets clustered in one area of the sky, while in others, they are scattered. How these are arranged and the distance between them indicates which govern the different aspects of our lives and personalities. These create a unique celestial blueprint, influencing our emotional, mental, and spiritual paths.

## Planets and Star Signs

Each planet in astrology is linked to specific zodiac signs and each planet's position in your birth chart adds complexity to how these influences manifest in your life, providing a deeper understanding of personal strengths, challenges, and life path. In modern astrology, which works with all nine planets, Scorpio, Aquarius, and Pisces are designated the outer planets.

- **Sun**: Rules Leo. Represents core identity, ego, and life purpose. Governs self-expression and vitality, affecting how we shine in the world.

- **Moon**: Rules Cancer. Influences emotions, instincts, and inner world. Shapes how we experience feelings, find comfort, and respond to life's ups and downs.

- **Mercury**: Rules Gemini and Virgo. Governs communication, thought processes, and intellect. Affects how we speak, think, and handle information, as well as problem-solving abilities.

- **Venus**: Rules Taurus and Libra. Represents love, beauty, and harmony. Influences relationships, attraction, values, and our sense of aesthetics.

- **Mars**: Rules Aries, and in traditional astrology, Scorpio. Governs action, desire, and drive. Affects how we pursue goals, assert ourselves, and deal with conflict.

- **Jupiter**: Rules Sagittarius, and in traditional astrology, Pisces. Symbolizes magnification, fortune, and expansion. Shapes how we seek knowledge, explore life's meaning, and approach opportunities for personal and spiritual growth.

- **Saturn**: Rules Capricorn, and in traditional astrology, Aquarius. Governs discipline, structure, and responsibility. Influences how we set boundaries, handle challenges, and pursue long-term goals.

- **Uranus**: Rules Aquarius. Represents innovation, rebellion, and change. Affects how we embrace new ideas, break away from the status quo, and seek personal freedom.

- **Neptune**: Rules Pisces. Governs dreams, intuition, and spirituality. Influences how we connect to the mystical, handle illusions, and seek emotional transcendence.

- **Pluto**: Represents change, power, and regeneration. Affects how we deal with deep changes, face fears, and confront the darker aspects of life for growth.

## *Planets in Detriment*

A planet is considered in detriment when it is in the sun sign opposite to the one it rules. You've discovered that the zodiac is divided into 12 equal portions or decanates, and you've seen that each sign has an opposite. A planet is in detriment when it is in your opposite sign. What it means is that the planet works counter (or opposite) to its natural tendencies, thus weakening its influence. This causes the planet's energies to feel restricted or less effective.

For instance, Mars rules Aries, which governs action and aggression. Aries opposite sign is Libra, which governs balance and diplomacy. Therefore, Mars is in detriment in Libra. While planets in detriment often require more conscious effort to harness their positive traits, it's not necessarily a bad thing, as they often provide balance. In the above example, Aries fiery disposition can be tempered by Libras peace, loving, and calming influence. On the other hand, if Libra can harness Mars' energy, they may learn to set boundaries, offsetting their gentle nature that often allows them to be taken for granted.

Here's a simple breakdown of planets in detriment:

- Sun: In detriment in Aquarius (opposite Leo). The sun's natural desire for self-expression is tempered by Aquarius' focus on collective ideals and independence.

- Moon: In detriment in Capricorn (opposite Cancer). Emotional expression (moon) can feel restricted or overly controlled in practical, disciplined Capricorn.

- Mercury: In detriment in Sagittarius and Pisces (opposite Gemini and Virgo). Mercury's clarity and focus on details may get muddled by Sagittarius' broad thinking or Pisces' emotional depth.

- Venus: In detriment in Aries and Scorpio (opposite Libra and Taurus). Venus' love for harmony may struggle with Aries assertiveness or Scorpio's deep intensity.

- Mars: In detriment in Libra and Taurus (opposite Aries and Scorpio). Mars' direct action is softened by Libra's diplomacy or Taurus' desire for stability.

- Jupiter: In detriment in Gemini and Virgo (opposite Sagittarius and Pisces). Jupiter's expansive, philosophical energy may get bogged down by Gemini's scattered curiosity or Virgo's analytical precision.

- Saturn: In detriment in Cancer and Leo (opposite Capricorn and Aquarius). Saturn's discipline feels constrained in Cancer's emotional world or Leo's need for recognition.

## *Retrograde Planets and Their Effects*

I'm sure you've heard mention of planets in retrograde. I've often heard radio personalities, friends, and astrologers speak about Mercury retrograde in particular. You may hear warnings when a planet goes into retrograde, and many face it with dread. However, a planet going into retrograde is a completely natural event and is no cause for alarm.

Rather, it's a time for introspection and reevaluation that should be embraced rather than met with resistance.

### *What Is a Planet in Retrograde?*

A planet in retrograde is caused by an optical illusion. It occurs when a planet appears to move backward in its orbit from our view on Earth. This is because of the differences in orbital speeds between Earth and the retrograde planet.

Retrogrades are thought to represent periods of reflection or disruption in the areas governed by the retrograde planet.

- Mercury: Disrupts communication, travel, and technology; encourages rethinking and reflection. Mercury is the most common retrograde and occurs 3–4 times a year for around 3 weeks.

- Venus: Affects relationships and finances; prompts revaluation of love, beauty, and values. Venus goes into retrograde approximately every 18 months for about 6 weeks.

- Mars: Reduces drive and energy; brings frustration in pursuing goals or conflicts. It goes into retrograde around every 2 years for around 2-2.5 months.

- Jupiter: Slows growth and expansion; fosters internal reflection on beliefs and opportunities. Jupiter is in retrograde once a year for around 4 months.

- Saturn: Challenges discipline and responsibility; highlights lessons and unresolved obligations. Similar to Jupiter, Saturn retrogrades occur once a year for about 4.5 months.

- Uranus: Causes sudden changes or disruptions; encourages internal innovation. Uranus goes into retrograde once a year for about 5 months.

- Neptune: Blurs clarity and intuition; inspires inner spiritual exploration. Neptune is in retrograde every year for about 5 months.

- Pluto: Triggers deep personal transformation and introspection on power dynamics. Again, this happens annually for about 5-6 months.

### *Stationary Planets*

When a planet is stationary, it means that the planet appears not to be moving. This is either because it is moving into a retrograde (stationary retrograde) or is resuming its normal forward (stationary direct) movement from Earth's perspective.

Depending on the planet, it can appear to be stationary for a few days, as in the case of Mercury, or several weeks, as with Mars.

This shift signals a time for moving forward with issues or areas influenced by the planet. For example, when Mercury stations direct after retrograde, communication and travel may start to flow more smoothly, and disruptions begin to clear up. It often marks a turning point for progress and clarity.

## *Asteroids and Their influence*

Asteroids in astrology represent different aspects of life that traditional planets may not cover.

Key asteroids include Chiron, Ceres, Juno, Pallas, and Vesta.

- **Juno**: Symbolizes marriage, commitment, and balance in relationships. It reveals how partnerships thrive through fairness and loyalty.

- **Chiron**: Known as the *wounded healer*, Chiron represents areas of deep pain and the potential for healing and wisdom through that suffering.

- **Ceres**: Governs nurturing, motherhood, and self-care. It highlights how we provide and receive nourishment, both physically and emotionally.

- **Pallas**: Represents wisdom, strategy, and ingenuity. It influences how we solve problems and approach life's challenges with resourcefulness.

- **Vesta**: Linked to spirituality and dedication, Vesta reflects focus, purity, and devotion to personal missions or causes, often tied to sacred work or home.

## The 12 Houses and Their Meanings

The 12 houses represent different areas of life, each governing specific traits and values. The placement of planets in these houses at the time of birth adds depth to a person's astrological chart, influencing how these themes manifest throughout life.

Each house is associated with a sign and its corresponding planet.

### *1. First House (House of Self)*

- Theme: Character, physical appearance, and public persona.

- Associated Sign: Aries. This house governs your self-image, personality, and how others perceive you. It reflects your personal style, demeanor, and how you approach new beginnings. Planets here shape your core identity and how you interact with the world.

## *2. Second House (House of Value)*

- Theme: Personal values, wealth, soft-skills, and self-image.
- Associated Sign: Taurus. This house deals with wealth, personal assets, and material security. It also represents your values and how you build self-esteem. The planets in this house show how you manage money and what makes you feel secure.

## *3. Third House (House of Communication)*

- Theme: Communication, reason, intelligence, and the natural world.
- Associated Sign: Gemini. The 3rd House governs how you think, learn, and communicate. It also relates to siblings, neighbors, and short trips. Planets here influence your mental agility, speech, and style of learning.

## *4. Fourth House (House of Home and Family)*

- Theme: Household, emotions, ancestry, family, and principles.
- Associated Sign: Cancer. This house is associated with your domestic life, early childhood, and sense of security. It governs the home you create for yourself and the influence of your family. Planets in this house show how you care for others as well as your self-care habits.

### *5. Fifth House (House of Pleasure)*

- Theme: Imagination, charm, and expressiveness.
- Associated Sign: Leo. The 5th House rules pleasure, creativity, and joyfulness. It is connected to romance, entertainment, hobbies, and children. Planets here reflect how you express yourself creatively and how you experience love and pleasure.

### *6. Sixth House (House of Health and Service)*

- Theme: Work, health, and everyday habits.
- Associated Sign: Virgo. This house focuses on work, service, health, and personal discipline. It covers how you maintain your physical well-being and manage day-to-day responsibilities. Planets in this house reveal your approach to work and how you maintain a healthy lifestyle.

### *7. Seventh House (House of Partnerships)*

- Theme: Relationships, joint effort, and alliances.
- Associated Sign: Libra. The 7th House governs one-on-one relationships, including marriage, business partnerships, and close friendships. It reflects your approach to commitment and what you seek in a partner. Planets here influence how you balance and cooperate with others.

### *8. Eighth House (House of Transformation)*

- Theme: Change, pooled resources, and intimacy.
- Associated Sign: Scorpio. This house is associated with deep emotional connections, joint finances, and personal

transformation. It governs birth, death, and rebirth cycles, along with matters of power and vulnerability. Planets here show how you handle intimacy and transformative experiences.

### *9. Ninth House (House of Philosophy)*

- Theme: Philosophy, tertiary education, and long-distance journeys.
- Associated Sign: Sagittarius. The 9th House represents the quest for knowledge, spirituality, and exploration of different cultures. It's linked to higher education, philosophy, and long journeys. Planets here influence your beliefs, travel experiences, and thirst for adventure.

### *10. Tenth House (House of Career and Public Life)*

- Theme: Profession, prestige, and long-term objectives.
- Associated Sign: Capricorn. This house governs your public life, career ambitions, and reputation. It represents your standing in society and the legacy you wish to leave. Planets here influence your career path, success, and how you achieve your life goals.

### *11. Eleventh House (House of Friendships and Social Networks)*

- Theme: Friendships, shared ideals, and future intentions.
- Associated Sign: Aquarius. The 11th House focuses on social connections and community involvement. It's also tied to your hopes and desires. Planets here affect how you relate to groups and envision your place within society.

## *12. Twelfth House (House of the Subconscious)*

- Theme: Spirituality, the unconscious, and hidden aspects of life.
- Associated Sign: Pisces. This house rules the unseen aspects of life, including the subconscious, dreams, and spirituality. It's associated with solitude, introspection, and hidden fears or strengths. Planets here reveal how you connect with your inner self and handle emotional baggage.

### *House Groups*

Houses are further divided into three groups based on their position and the role they play in a birth chart. Together, these groups of houses provide balance in a birth chart, influencing both action and reflection.

- Angular Houses (1st, 4th, 7th, 10th)
    - These are the most powerful houses, representing action and life-defining areas such as identity, home, relationships, and career.
    - Planets in angular houses tend to have a strong and direct influence, often shaping major events or characteristics in a person's life.
- Succedent Houses (2nd, 5th, 8th, 11th)
    - These houses follow the angular ones and deal with stability, resources, and development. They relate to possessions, creativity, transformation, and friendships.
    - Planets here influence how we build and maintain security and resources, contributing to growth and persistence in specific life areas.

- Cadent Houses (3rd, 6th, 9th, 12th)
    - Cadent houses are linked to adaptability, learning, and transition. They govern communication, health, higher learning, and the subconscious.
    - Planets in cadent houses encourage reflection, movement, and transformation, affecting how we adapt to changes and process experiences.

## *How the Houses Impact Different Areas of Your Life*

Each house represents a vital area of life, and the placement of planets in these houses bring their unique energy into those areas and adds layers of meaning. Furthermore, each planet's influence depends on their position within the 12 houses of the chart, shaping personal strengths, challenges, and opportunities for growth.

To explain, Mercury placed in the 3rd House (communication) may enhance one's ability to learn and articulate ideas, while Venus in the 7th House (relationships) could emphasize harmonious partnerships.

Additionally, aspects between planets influence how their energies combine or conflict, further refining the chart's overall effect. Planets positioned near the ascendant (the 1st House) often exert a strong influence over personality and outward behavior, while those near the midheaven (10th House) shape public life and career paths.

This dynamic interplay between planets and houses creates a unique astrological blueprint for each person, offering insight into life's patterns and potential challenges.

## Progression Quiz

1. **What is a birth chart in astrology?**

    a. A map of where all the planets were in their journey around the sun at the exact moment you were born.

    b. A prediction of your future based on your date of birth.

    c. A list of all your past lives and their astrological signs.

    d. The alignment of stars at the time of your birth.

2. **Which planet represents communication, intellect, and expression in astrology?**

    a. Mars

    b. Venus

    c. Mercury

    d. Jupiter

3. **What is the significance of asteroids in astrology?**

    a. They determine your physical appearance.

    b. They represent minor influences that can reveal more about personal narratives and patterns.

    c. They are responsible for major life events.

    d. They indicate wealth and prosperity.

4. **What does each house in an astrological chart represent?**

    a. The 12 months of the year.

    b. Different aspects or areas of an individual's life.

c. The 12 zodiac signs.

d. Your personality traits.

5. **Which sign is associated with being practical, ambitious, and disciplined?**

   a. Gemini

   b. Capricorn

   c. Libra

   d. Scorpio

## *Answers*

1. a. A map of where all the planets were in their journey around the sun at the exact moment you were born.
2. c. Mercury
3. b. They represent minor influences that can reveal more about personal narratives and patterns.
4. b. Different aspects or areas of an individual's life.
5. b. Capricorn

Chapter 4:

# Birth Chart: A Deeper Look

You now have a basic understanding of how birth charts work, the effects of the planets, and how the 12 houses potentially affect your character and life in general.

We also have other celestial positions and bodies to consider when forming a chart. Among these are aspects, orbs, and lunar nodes.

# Aspects

Aspects refer to the angles formed between planets in a birth chart, influencing how their energies interact and the result of these in a birth chart. There are several aspects which represent relationships between different planetary forces and can reveal harmony, tension, or challenges in our lives.

Soft aspects, like trines and sextiles, promote harmony and ease. They allow the planets involved to work together smoothly, fostering collaboration and positive outcomes. For example, a trine between Venus and Jupiter could suggest luck in love, making these connections feel effortless and beneficial.

Hard aspects, such as squares and oppositions, introduce tension and challenges. They often create friction, pushing us to confront difficulties and grow from them. While hard aspects can be uncomfortable, they also provide opportunities for personal development and deeper self-awareness.

## *Major Planetary Aspects*

Conjunctions, oppositions, and trines are types of aspects; these are relationships between planets that influence how their energies interact and their effect on our birth charts.

### *Conjunctions*

When two or more planets are in the same zodiac sign, typically within 0-10 degrees of each other, they form a conjunction. They indicate areas of strength and intensity.

- The planets' energies blend together, intensifying their influence. Conjunctions can be powerful and focused, amplifying both the positive and negative traits of the planets involved. For example, a conjunction between the sun and

Mercury enhances communication and mental clarity but may also lead to an overly analytical mindset.

- This aspect fosters a sense of unity and heightened energy, but the outcome depends heavily on the planets and signs involved.

### *Oppositions*

Oppositions occur when two planets are directly across from each other in the zodiac, 180 degrees apart. They indicate where you may come across difficulties.

- This aspect creates tension and polarity, as the planets pull in opposite directions. Oppositions require balance and compromise, as the contrasting energies can cause internal or external conflict. For instance, an opposition between Mars (assertiveness) and Venus (harmony) may challenge how we balance personal desires with relationships.

- Oppositions encourage growth by forcing us to integrate opposing forces, leading to greater awareness and harmony through conflict resolution.

### *Trines*

A trine forms when two planets are 120 degrees apart, usually in the same element (fire, earth, air, or water). These show areas where natural flow is predominant.

- Trines are harmonious aspects that allow the planets' energies to flow smoothly, creating ease and natural talent in the areas they govern. Trines support personal growth without much effort, but they can also make one complacent due to the lack of challenge. For example, a trine between the moon and Venus can bring emotional stability and an effortless expression of love and beauty.

- Trines represent natural talents or blessings, but they require awareness to avoid stagnation due to their ease.

### *Square*

A square forms when two planets are at a 90-degree angle from each other and they are separated by three sun signs. For instance, if a planet is in Aries, whatever planet is in Cancer would form a square aspect.

- Squares create tension and conflict between two planets, creating friction that often drives personal growth through challenge.
- The friction forces growth and change, as it pushes you to confront obstacles and work through difficulties.

### *Sextile*

A sextile is formed when two planets are 60 degrees apart from each other they are two sun signs away from one another. For instance, if a planet is in Taurus, another planet in Pisces or Cancer would create a sextile.

- A sextile represents a supportive and harmonious connection between planets, fostering cooperation and opportunity. The effect is subtler than that of a trine.
- It encourages opportunities for cooperation, creativity, and learning, often resulting in positive outcomes, although this requires conscious effort and initiative.

These interactions shape how a person expresses their planetary energies throughout life.

## *Minor Planetary Aspects*

Minor aspects offer subtle yet significant influences on a person's chart. Though less powerful than major aspects, they highlight hidden patterns and contribute to self-awareness and personal growth.

### *Semi-Square*

Formed when two planets are 45 degrees apart. This is half the distance of a square (90°), so the planets are one and a half signs apart.

- Represents mild inner conflict or frustration. It signals smaller, manageable challenges that push for slow but necessary changes in behavior or circumstances.

### *Quincunx or Inconjunct*

Occurs when two planets are 150 degrees apart, and are usually five signs away from each other.

- Reflects areas of imbalance between planets. The energies here are disconnected, requiring ongoing adjustments to create harmony between conflicting parts of life.

### *Semi-Sextile*

The result of two planets being 30 degrees apart and one sign away from each other. It's a gentle aspect, signaling subtle cooperation between the planets' energies.

- Indicates subtle support or cooperation between planets. This aspect promotes quiet opportunities for growth, but you need to consciously harness its potential to notice progress.

### *Sesquiquadrate*

Formed when two planets are 135 degrees apart, halfway between a square (90°) and an opposition (180°).

- Similar to a square, but less intense, this aspect indicates minor tension or irritation. It often calls attention to unresolved issues that need small adjustments over time.

### *Quintile*

Formed when two planets are 72 degrees apart, usually located about two and a half signs away from each other.

- (72°): Associated with inventiveness, flair, and inspiration. This aspect highlights areas of life like creativity and talent where there is a unique gift or an unconventional way of thinking, promoting personal expression and artistic abilities.

## Orbs

When astrologers examine a birth chart, they assess how planets interact based on their positions and the angles between them. An orb is the allowable distance, in degrees, between two planets when forming an aspect. For example, if two planets are five degrees apart and the aspect is considered to have an orb of seven degrees, the aspect is still influential.

For a better understanding, I found that what helped me was to picture a planet's orb as being similar to how the moon appears when it has a halo surrounding it. It doesn't really have a halo, but it almost looks as though the moon is extending itself.

### Orb Ranges

The ranges of influence are categorized in three main ranges.

- Tight Orbs: Between 0-3 degrees. This indicates a strong, immediate influence between planets.
- Moderate Orbs: Around 4-7 degrees. This influence is still relevant but less intense.
- Wide Orbs: 8 degrees or more. The influence diminishes significantly but can still be noted.

The position of orbs in our birth offer insight into areas of enhanced, tension, or balance. They may be subtle, in the case of wide orbs, but are nonetheless considered by astrologers when examining a birth chart.

- Enhanced: The more planets that are within orb of each other, the richer the interpretation. For example, if Venus (representing love) is in a tight trine with Jupiter (representing luck), it suggests a strong potential for happy and beneficial relationships.
- Tension: Conversely, if Mars (representing aggression) is in a close square with Saturn (representing restriction), this could indicate challenges or internal conflicts.
- Subtle Influences: Wider orbs may bring in subtler effects that can manifest later in life or in specific situations rather than as immediate traits.

## Lunar Nodes

You may have heard of lunar nodes or shadow planets. In Vedic astrology they are referred to as *Rahu* and *Ketu*, and in Western astrology, they are known as the North Node, or Dragon's head, and the South Node, or Dragon's tail. These are not actual planets but rather points at which the moon's orbit crosses the sun's path. The eclipses we experience through the year are indications of the lunar nodes intersecting the sun's path.

I love mythology regarding the heavens, and here's a short version of how Rahu and Ketu came into being:

There was a time when the gods (devas) and demons (asuras) wanted obtain Amrita, the nectar of immortality. In order to do so, they had to work together churning the cosmic ocean to bring it to the surface. Lord Vishnu wanted to maintain universal balance so he took the form of the beautiful goddess Mohini and began distributing the nectar only to the gods, deceiving the demons.

However, one demon, named Swarbhanu, disguised himself as a god and sat between the Sun (Surya) and the Moon (Chandra) to drink the nectar. Surya and Chandra recognized him and alerted Lord Vishnu, who cut off the demon's head. Since Swarbhanu had already consumed some nectar, he was immortal and his head and body transformed into two separate entities: Rahu, the head, and Ketu, the body.

Rahu and Ketu became celestial beings, with Rahu symbolizing the dragon's head and Ketu the tail. They are considered shadow planets that influence eclipses; Rahu causes solar eclipses by swallowing Surya, while Ketu is responsible for lunar eclipses. Their positions in a person's astrological chart signify karmic lessons and spiritual growth.

Lunar nodes are positioned directly opposite from each other and move in retrograde constantly. Because the nodes' path is at an angle, the North Node always appears to be moving upwards, with the opposite South Node moving at a downward angle. Think of a rolling ball: The top is always moving down as it rolls forward, and the bottom rotates upwards.

- **North Node (Dragon's Head)**: The North Node represents the future you are destined to embrace including what you should strive for and the lessons to learn in this lifetime. This can feel daunting, as it's unfamiliar territory. Think of it like stepping into a new chapter of life, such as starting a new venture; it's an opportunity to reinvent yourself and shape your identity. Similarly, the North Node's energy invites you to embrace transformation and creativity, allowing you to evolve and shape your reality as you move forward into new experiences. It has a similar nature to that of Jupiter, which is about expansion and growth.

- **South Node (Dragon's Tail)**: The South Node reflects the experiences, energies, habits, and relationships tied to your past or even your past lives. It represents karmic patterns we've already lived through and now need to release. These familiar emotions can give us a sense of déjà vu, showing what we're holding onto that no longer serves our growth. By recognizing these recurring thoughts and behaviors, we can consciously move away from them, allowing ourselves to break free from outdated cycles and move forward in this lifetime. It has similar characteristics to Saturn, which is associated with past actions and karma.

## *How Nodes Influence Your Life*

Approximately every 18.6 months, the lunar nodes shift into new signs. In our birth charts, these shifting placements reveal insights into our past paths and present life direction.

### *North Node in Aries/South Node in Libra*

When in Aries, there's an emphasis on embracing independence and authentic self-expression, moving away from the desire to please others. This personal growth journey is particularly significant for those with the North Node in Aries, who are encouraged to assert their individuality confidently.

It's important to prioritize self-reliance over relationships, avoiding the tendency to let partnerships define one's identity. Although breaking free from unhealthy relationships may require effort and perseverance, it is achievable with determination.

### *North Node in Taurus/South Node in Scorpio*

If your North Node is in Taurus, your purpose in this life centers on building a secure and self-reliant foundation. Your journey involves achieving financial independence and freeing yourself from any toxic dependencies.

In past incarnations, symbolized by your South Node in Scorpio, you may have faced themes of loss and reliance on others. Now, you're called to take charge, especially regarding your financial well-being, and foster emotional steadiness. Strive to avoid excess and isolation, staying receptive to meaningful connections while maintaining your authenticity.

### *North Node in Gemini/South Node in Sagittarius*

If your North Node is in Gemini, your life path involves mastering communication and human connection. Representing close relationships and community, Gemini's energy encourages you to focus on building bonds where you are and making a local impact. With your South Node in Sagittarius, past lives may have centered around exploration and seeking knowledge. Now, your journey is about simplifying complex thoughts, engaging with others, and learning to articulate your ideas clearly, whether through public speaking, writing, or other forms of expression.

### *North Node in Cancer/South Node in Capricorn*

Having a Cancer North Node means your journey in this life is centered around fostering deep emotional bonds, cultivating a sense of family, and creating a nurturing home environment. In contrast, your South Node in Capricorn reflects past lifetimes focused on ambition, hard work, and providing for others, often at the cost of neglecting your own emotional needs. While you may be naturally driven by career and success, this lifetime calls for embracing vulnerability, prioritizing self-care, and deepening your relationships.

By nurturing empathy and meaningful connections, both your personal and professional life will flourish.

### *North Node in Leo/South Node in Aquarius*

With your North Node in Leo, your life's mission is to step into the spotlight, embracing joy, self-expression, and personal confidence. In contrast, your South Node in Aquarius reflects past lives where you put collective needs above your own. Now, the focus shifts to prioritizing your happiness, healing your inner child, and unlocking your creative potential. You are meant to lead with charisma and self-assurance, leaving a lasting impact through your unique artistic contributions. This path encourages unapologetic self-fulfillment and the celebration of your creative spirit.

### *North Node in Virgo/South Node in Pisces*

If your North Node is in Virgo, your life's purpose revolves around grounding yourself and serving society through practical means. Achieving this requires you to adopt a more communicative, critical, and assertive mindset. Your South Node in Pisces suggests past lives centered on spirituality and creativity, but this lifetime calls for a balance between dreams and tangible reality. By honing your skills in fields like healthcare, science, or problem-solving, you can turn your idealistic visions into impactful, concrete contributions that meet the needs of the world around you.

### *North Node in Libra/South Node in Aries*

Those with the North Node in Libra find their sense of fulfillment in nurturing harmonious relationships. They are encouraged to embrace cooperation, think carefully before they act, and welcome compromise. Although their natural tendency is to prioritize their own needs, they are on a journey of peaceful negotiation and interaction. They often struggle between their yearning for connection and their need for independence.

The primary challenge they face is striking a balance between remaining true to their authentic selves and being accommodating to others.

### *North Node in Scorpio/South Node in Taurus*

With a North Node in Scorpio, your purpose is to explore the deep mysteries of life and gain control over your experiences rather than just seeking material wealth. Having a South Node in Taurus suggests past lives focused on luxury, leading to a boredom with superficial pleasures. In this lifetime, embrace richer connections and take emotional and financial risks, finding freedom in the unknown. While you may tend toward obsession, this intensity can help you manage others' affairs. Trust your instincts and be patient on this transformative journey.

### *North Node in Sagittarius/South Node in Gemini*

With the North Node in Sagittarius, your journey focuses on exploration and sharing your wisdom. This fire sign encourages you to expand your horizons through travel and new experiences. Having a South Node in Gemini indicates past lives spent in social circles and local drama. Now, you're called to express bold ideas and challenge norms. While your South Node may pull you toward others' expectations, your North Node inspires you to foster creativity and open-mindedness. Use your communication skills to make a meaningful impact as a teacher and philosopher.

### *North Node in Capricorn/South Node in Cancer*

If your North Node is in Capricorn, you are called to work hard and develop your career as a strong leader, especially in business. Your South Node in Cancer suggests past lives focused on nurturing, which may hinder your ability to assert yourself publicly. While you have great potential for success, it might take time to realize it, as those with this placement often achieve later in life.

To grow, focus on building emotional resilience and meaningful connections while stepping into your leadership role.

### *North Node in Aquarius/South Node in Leo*

If your North Node is in Aquarius, your journey focuses on challenging norms and empowering others to create a better world. With a South Node in Leo, past lives centered around self-love and fame, giving you natural charisma. Now, you're called to move beyond self-indulgence and uplift your community. You have the potential to be a revolutionary leader or advocate for societal change, emphasizing collective goals over personal gain. While you may struggle with selfishness, your mission is to foster unity and envision a brighter future for all.

### *North Node in Pisces/South Node in Virgo*

If your North Node is in Pisces, you may feel challenged by ideas that lack logic and proof. With a South Node in Virgo, past lives focused on practicality, leading to a rational mindset. This lifetime encourages you to provide emotional support rather than fix problems. Embrace love and spirituality, trusting your intuition over logic. Your path involves accepting what you can't control and unlocking your potential as a spiritual healer or artist, bridging the material and spiritual worlds, despite struggles with boundaries and perfectionism.

## Progression Quiz

1. **What are the major aspects in astrology?**

    a. Conjunction, Sextile, Square, Trine, Opposition

    b. Sun, Moon, Mars, Venus

c. Aries, Taurus, Gemini

d. Ascendant, Descendant

2. **In astrology terms, what does *retrograde* refer to?**

   a. When a planet appears to be moving backward in its orbit from Earth's perspective.

   b. When a planet is at its closest point to the sun.

   c. The time when the moon is not visible from Earth.

   d. The alignment of three or more planets.

3. **What are lunar nodes in astrology?**

   a. The points where the moon's orbit crosses the ecliptic.

   b. The phase of the moon.

   c. A type of aspect between two planets.

   d. A term used for when a planet changes signs.

4. **What does an *orb* refer to in astrology?**

   a. It refers to how far apart two planets are from each other within an aspect.

   b. It refers to the circular path that planets take around the sun.

   c. It refers to the shape of a birth chart.

   d. It refers to a specific type of astrological prediction.

5. **What is a progressed chart in astrology?**

   a. A method used by astrologers that progresses your natal chart forward one day for every year after your birth.

b. A detailed map of all planetary positions at any given moment.

c. An advanced technique for predicting future events based on planetary movements.

d. The chart that shows your potential and opportunities throughout life.

## *Answers*

1. a. Conjunction, Sextile, Square, Trine, Opposition
2. a. When a planet appears to be moving backward in its orbit from Earth's perspective.
3. a. The points where the moon's orbit crosses the ecliptic.
4. a. It refers to how far apart two planets are from each other within an aspect.
5. a. A method used by astrologers that progresses your natal chart forward one day for every year after your birth.

Chapter 5:

# Spiritual and Personal Growth

Astrology goes beyond mere predictions; it's a profound guide for understanding yourself and fostering personal growth. By examining your birth chart, you can identify strengths and weaknesses, align your goals with astrological cycles, and improve relationships.

A strong Mars, for instance, can indicate high energy and motivation, while a difficult Saturn-sun aspect may highlight struggles with authority or self-discipline, and transits like Jupiter's can bring opportunities.

Staying aware of these influences allows you to focus on areas ripe for improvement and embrace changes for a more fulfilling life.

## Self-Discovery and Development

By working with an astrologer, you can gain a personalized understanding of these dynamics. For example, if your chart reveals a tendency to be overly critical, you can work on developing self-compassion and becoming more constructive in criticism of yourself and others.

- **Discover Strengths and Weaknesses**: By exploring your birth chart, you can gain a clear picture of your personality traits, helping you use your strengths and address areas where you can improve.

- **Navigate Challenges**: Astrology highlights potential challenges and provides direction during difficult events by offering personalized advice based on your chart.

- **Improve Relationships**: Astrology provides insights into relationship dynamics and compatibility, leading to better understanding, communication, and emotional balance in both personal and professional relationships.

- **Facilitate Growth**: Use astrology to pinpoint areas for self-improvement, offering strategies that align with your unique personality traits.

- **Discover Life's Purpose**: The placement of the sun, moon, and ascendant reveals your life's mission, offering direction for both personal and professional growth.

- **Navigate Life's Timing**: Your birth chart can reveal important life cycles and events and help you make better decisions during these periods.

- **Set and Achieve Goals**: Astrological events, such as planetary transits and lunar phases, can inform the timing of your goals, like starting new ventures during the new moon or taking the time to reflect during Saturn returns.

- **Opportunities for Growth**: Astrological transits, such as Jupiter's influence on your sun, bring opportunities for expansion and optimism, encouraging personal development. Aligning your objectives with these could help you achieve success in certain areas.

- **Mindful Awareness**: Astrology encourages mindfulness through daily reflections and personalized horoscopes, cultivating a deeper understanding of yourself and your place in the world.

- **Professional Guidance**: Consulting with an astrologer offers personalized insights into your birth chart, helping you navigate life's complexities with tailored advice.

## The Moon Plays a Part

The moon, as we know, affects our water systems on Earth. Many people believe that we are affected by the moon; some more than others. While science doesn't support the theory completely, I have a relative who definitely is affected by the moon, and we noticed this behavior when she was still a small child.

I know a health worker at a major hospital who says that nobody likes working over a full moon because of the increase in trauma cases. From an astrological viewpoint, the moon definitely affects us and should be considered.

The moon sign acts as the foundation of our emotional life, instinctual behavior, and internal comfort mechanisms. It guides how we experience feelings, what we need for emotional fulfillment, and the type of environments or relationships that offer us security.

Understanding our moon sign can show us our deeper emotional needs, shaping our journey toward emotional balance and inner serenity.

## *Emotional Nature*

- Reflection of Feelings: The moon governs how we experience and express emotions. While the sun sign shapes conscious goals and ego, the moon sign reflects our emotional reactions and needs. For example, a Cancer moon will have a deep, nurturing emotional nature, craving security and close connections, while an Aquarius moon might express emotions more intellectually or detached.

- Emotional Expression: Moon signs influence how openly or reservedly feelings are shared. Fire and air moon signs tend to express emotions more outwardly and actively while water and earth moons are more introspective or cautious in emotional expression.

## *Instincts and Inner World*

- Instinctual Reactions: The moon reflects our natural instincts and how we react to stress, intimacy, and personal experiences. It shows our gut responses to emotional situations. A Taurus moon, for instance, may seek physical comfort and consistency, while a Sagittarius moon instinctively looks for freedom and space to avoid feeling trapped.

- Subconscious Desires: Our deepest desires, especially ones related to emotional satisfaction, are governed by the moon. It governs our innate patterns, often passed down through family or early life experiences. Someone with a Scorpio moon might crave emotional intensity and deep transformation, seeking control over their emotional life.

## *Emotional Needs and Security*

- Emotional Fulfillment: The moon sign reveals what we need to feel emotionally satisfied and secure. For instance, a Capricorn moon may need structure, discipline, and achievement to feel emotionally grounded, while a Pisces moon requires a sense of emotional connection, creativity, and spiritual fulfillment.

- Comfort and Coping Mechanisms: The moon shows how a person seeks comfort during stress or hardship. A Gemini moon may find solace in communication or intellectual stimulation, whereas a Virgo moon seeks comfort through order and productivity.
- Nurturing and Security: The moon relates to how we nurture others and how we wish to be nurtured. Someone with a Libra moon may find security in harmonious relationships, while an Aries moon may feel secure through personal independence and assertiveness.

### *Finding Comfort and Emotional Stability*

- Restoring Emotional Balance: Each moon sign has specific needs for emotional balance and security. Water signs like Cancer, Scorpio, and Pisces require emotional depth, intuition, and empathy, while earth signs like Taurus, Virgo, and Capricorn rely on stability, routine, and tangible results to feel secure. Fire and air signs, on the other hand, may need adventure, intellectual stimulation, or social connection to regain emotional balance.

## Black Moon Lilith Signs

Lilith, a mythological figure, is often regarded as the first woman to embody independence. A controversial figure, some view her as a powerful goddess, while others see her as a dark and malevolent spirit. In Jewish folklore, Lilith is said to have been Adam's first wife (although there is no mention of this in the scriptures), who refused to be submissive to him, leading to her exile from the Garden of Eden.

Over time, Lilith became a symbol of shadowy feminine energy, frequently depicted as a fearsome figure that men found intimidating. In some tales, she is portrayed as a demoness driven by envy, preying on young mothers and brides, while other accounts emphasize her seductive and destructive powers over men. Despite these negative portrayals, Lilith's story also offers themes of self-empowerment, healing, and spiritual transformation.

In astrology, her placement can reveal hidden strengths and unresolved anger, offering insight into one's deeper emotional and spiritual journey. Lilith, or Black Moon Lilith, represents the hidden, suppressed aspects of your personality, often linked to those desires and feelings you keep secret to avoid judgment. It is connected to the farthest point of the moon's orbit from Earth, symbolizing the darker, raw, and primal side of feminine energy.

Lilith's placement in your birth chart highlights themes of independence, rebellion, and areas where you resist conformity. It also touches on challenges related to sexuality, fear, anger, and rejection, offering insights into deep psychological growth.

## *Aries*

You are a fiercely independent spirit, who thrives on breaking boundaries and forging your own path. You possess a powerful, confident energy that can have you taking bold, decisive actions. While your determination often leads to success, it may also result in a tendency to be overly competitive or impulsive.

To heal your Lilith in Aries, focus on accepting your vulnerabilities and flaws; your individuality and authenticity make you unique. Learning to accept and love all parts of yourself will encourage personal growth and fulfillment.

## *Taurus*

Lilith in Taurus represents a deep connection to indulgence and earthly pleasures. You're drawn to sensory experiences and have a desire for comfort and security, often working hard to attain the luxuries you crave. Once you focus on a goal, your drive is unstoppable. However, you may find it difficult to rely on others.

The challenge for Lilith in Taurus is to embrace vulnerability, allowing yourself to open up and trust others while softening your protective instincts.

### *Gemini*

You embody quick-witted, dynamic energy, especially when it comes to love and communication. You're naturally curious and thrive on intellectually stimulating conversations, which draws others to you in social settings.

Your ability to communicate at all levels enables you to connect with many people, but you may keep things superficial to avoid being vulnerable. This can prevent you from forming deep emotional bonds.

Learning to balance your charm with authentic expression is key to fostering meaningful relationships and embracing the full spectrum of your communicative power.

### *Cancer*

When Lilith is in Cancer, it brings heightened intuition and emotional sensitivity. You are highly empathetic, although deep emotional connections may lead you to over-give in relationships. You often avoid direct confrontation by directing your emotions in less effective ways.

To grow with Lilith placed here, it's important to assert your worth, set clear boundaries, and engage in open, honest communication instead of using your passive-aggressive tendencies. Finding balance in your emotional world will help you feel more empowered.

## *Leo*

You are a commanding, radiant personality that draws attention naturally. You are the picture of confidence, but this can lead to self-absorption or a fear of being vulnerable and losing control in love. Past relationships may have involved partners who were jealous or diminished your light.

Your spiritual growth lies in partnerships where both you and your partner can express yourselves fully and shine together without fear. It's about balancing your individuality with the willingness to share love openly.

## *Virgo*

There is a strong need for control, structure, and perfection when Lilith appears here. You appear highly organized and disciplined, though it often comes from intense self-discipline and effort. You may be overly critical or controlling, especially in relationships, out of fear of rejection or inadequacy. Your standards for yourself and others can sometimes be unreasonable, which can limit your sense of fulfillment.

Embracing the imperfections of life and love and allowing for flexibility is key to finding balance and happiness.

## *Libra*

You seek equilibrium and peace in life, but the temptation to indulge can sometimes lead you astray. Your magnetic feminine energy makes you naturally captivating, drawing new opportunities and relationships with ease. Others are often drawn to your charm and success. Despite this, you frequently find yourself preoccupied with others' opinions, leading to comparisons and self-centered tendencies.

To nurture more fulfilling connections, focus on compassion and allow relationships to evolve naturally. Remember that love isn't a competition.

## *Scorpio*

You radiate an intense and magnetic energy, with an undeniable presence that commands attention. You exude confidence and aren't hesitant to leverage your charm and allure to reach your ambitions. Scorpios are generally thought of as being deep which intrigues others. They are naturally drawn to your power and often want to be close to it. Because past partners may have tried to suppress your light or control you, you tend to be guarded and hide your true self.

Embrace your authenticity; by being open and honest, you'll find that real love won't hold your past against you.

## *Sagittarius*

If Lilith resides in Sagittarius, you embody the free-spirited and adventurous flirt of the zodiac. Naturally curious with an open heart, you're always eager to dive into new experiences, radiating a vibrant and magnetic energy that draws people to you. While you enjoy the attention, commitment isn't your top priority and even traditional relationships or dating may make you feel caged. The thought of settling down might stir feelings of restlessness, and sometimes, your indecision can have you missing out on meaningful opportunities.

To truly grow, challenge your views on love and learn to embrace the thrill of the unknown.

## *Capricorn*

You have a deep drive for accomplishment, status, and success. You take great pride in your disciplined work ethic and always aim to surpass the targets you set for yourself. Yet, when it comes to love, you may prefer a traditional, even rigid, approach, which can make you seem emotionally distant. While holding to your standards is important, you need to allow room for flexibility and openness. Don't let your need for perfection prevent you from enjoying life and taking time to relax.

Step back, reconnect with your own needs and desires, and let go of the need to live up to other people's expectations.

## *Aquarius*

With Lilith in Aquarius, you embody the spirit of the rebellious visionary. Fearlessly outspoken, you're not shy about voicing your unique and unconventional ideas. In love, your mysterious and unpredictable nature adds an irresistible allure, and you thrive on the excitement of new experiences and shared adventures. Yet, beneath this boldness, there's a lingering fear of being judged for your differences, which can lead you to hide your true self and put your guard up. This can cause emotional distance in relationships.

To deepen your connections, release the doubts about your self-worth and unapologetically embrace your authenticity.

## *Pisces*

You have a profound sense of romanticism and spiritual depth. You have a natural gift for creating deep emotional connections, often understanding others on an almost intuitive level. There's a graceful, effortless charm to your presence that draws people in, but your idealistic view on love may result in complicated situations. This optimistic, even naive, outlook may cause you to overlook reality and self-centered behavior.

Remember not to lose yourself in relationships; set and maintain healthy boundaries to preserve your identity and find true happiness.

## Rare Planetary Features

### *Yods*

A Yod in astrology, also called the *Finger of God*, is a rare planetary alignment involving three planets forming a tall triangle. Two planets are in a sextile (harmonious) aspect at 60° and two sun signs apart. Both of these form a quincunx (uncomfortable) aspect at 150° with a third apex planet positioned five sun signs apart. This creates friction and challenges in the chart, symbolizing intense spiritual lessons, destiny, and the need for constant adjustment. The Yod represents unique spiritual assignments and the breaking of ancestral or karmic patterns.

### *Grand Trines*

A grand trine occurs in a birth chart when three planets align to form an equilateral triangle, all within the same element (fire, earth, air, or water). These planets are spaced 120 degrees apart, forming harmonious trine aspects. A grand trine is considered an auspicious aspect, where the planets interact smoothly, amplifying their energy. Depending on the element, the grand trine can emphasize creativity (fire), practicality (earth), intellectualism (air), or emotional depth (water), giving us an inherent sense of balance and ease in these areas of life.

### *Stellium*

Stelliums allows you to understand yourself better by showing you your weaknesses, strengths, and the things you need to work on.

The first is the acceptance of who you are and where you can improve. Our birth chart gives us a lifetime to learn and become aware of where we need growth and how to accomplish it.

People who have a stellium appearing in their chart may sometimes come across as rigid and stubborn. These placements can reinforce their beliefs, while also allowing them to be open-minded about differing viewpoints, although these will be closely examined and analyzed. Changing perceptions is no easy task and takes convincing and effort.

Stelliums show us where to focus and what needs to be worked on. With their concentrated influence, they can allow us to become more self-aware and in touch with who we are. Stelliums influence our reactions and responses in various scenarios. If you don't feel entirely "at home" in your sun sign, you may be influenced by a stellium in your chart.

## *Square*

Squares occur when two planets are 90 degrees apart and share the same astrological quality (cardinal, fixed, or mutable), creating tension and friction. This aspect often leads to conflict, with both sides digging in their heels, resisting compromise, and engaging in power struggles. However, resolving these conflicts requires finding balance through self-awareness and flexibility. If your chart contains squares, they highlight areas of inner tension and personal growth. A T-Square forms when three planets are involved, while a Grand Square involves four planets, intensifying the challenges.

- **T-Square**: A T-Square forms when three planets are in a tense configuration, each at 90-degree angles, creating a dynamic struggle where one planet mediates between the other two. This aspect pushes us to make decisions and face unresolved issues, often with an urgent, forceful energy. In a T-Square, all planets share the same quality (cardinal, mutable, or fixed), and the missing fourth sign offers a way to restore balance. People with a T-Square in their chart may feel pulled in different directions but can channel this tension into either struggling with completion or driving themselves toward success.

- **Grand Square**: Also called a *Grand Cross*, is a rare and intense astrological aspect, occurring when four planets form 90-degree angles (squares) and oppose each other. This alignment creates significant tension, with competing energies demanding balance and resolution. Each planet involved shares the same astrological quality—cardinal, fixed, or mutable—indicating the theme of the challenge. Whether focused on leadership (cardinal), change (mutable), or security (fixed), a Grand Cross requires negotiation and collaboration. Those with a Grand Cross in their charts often face powerful challenges but also possess immense potential for growth.

Astrology offers a window of opportunity in different areas of our lives by shedding light on where we can or what we need to work on for personal development.

Some of these are explored in the coming chapters.

## Progression Quiz

1. **What is the primary purpose of astrology in terms of personal growth?**

    a. Predicting future events.

    b. Understanding personality traits and life patterns.

    c. Choosing the best career path.

    d. Finding a suitable life partner.

2. **What does Black Moon Lilith in an astrological chart represent?**

    a. The darkest aspects of our personality.

    b. Our financial prosperity.

c. Our past lives.

d. Our communication skills.

**3. In astrology, what do midheaven and Imum Coeli signify?**

a. Love and relationships.

b. Career and home life respectively.

c. Public image and private self respectively.

d. Health issues.

**4. What is a Yod formation in an astrological chart?**

a. A beneficial aspect that brings luck.

b. A challenging configuration often called *Finger of God.*

c. An alignment that signifies great wealth.

d. A sign of impending illness.

**5. What does a grand trine represent in astrology?**

a. It represents challenges or obstacles to overcome.

b. It signifies good fortune and talent.

c. It indicates health problems.

d. It shows areas where you may struggle with learning.

## *Answers*

1. b. Understanding personality traits and life patterns.
2. a. The darkest aspects of our personality.
3. c. Public image and private self respectively.
4. b. A challenging configuration often called *Finger of God.*
5. b. It signifies good fortune and talent.

Chapter 6:

# Decision-Making With Astrology

While your birth chart shows the planetary positions at the time of your birth, transits reflect the current movements of planets and how they interact with your natal chart. As planets journey through the zodiac, they form aspects with your birth planets, influencing your life.

Progressions, on the other hand, represent long-term growth, with each day after birth symbolizing a year of life. Together, transits and progressions provide insight into potential events and personal development based on your chart's unique strengths and challenges.

# Planetary Transits

A transit refers to the movement of planets as they journey through the zodiac and interact with the planets in your birth chart. The influence of a transit varies based on which planets are involved and how they connect to your natal planets. They also create a shift in energy that resonates with the theme of the particular house it passes through.

These movements can affect many areas of life, such as personal issues, relationships, and major decisions. We use transits to anticipate key life events and shifts, offering insight into potential changes and opportunities.

By interpreting these transits, we can align our actions with cosmic energies and enhance our decision making. Instead of trying to control outcomes, we can use various transits to help us navigate life's challenges better through timing planned events to fit in with the movements in our skies.

## *Minor Planetary Transits*

Minor transits are the movements of the celestial bodies that lie between the sun and Earth, known as the *inner planets*, and include the moon and the sun. They are also called *personal planets*. As these pass through the sun signs, they form brief interactions with the planets in our birth chart. These transits influence daily, weekly, or monthly emotions, thoughts, and minor events, bringing subtle changes in mood, communication, or relationships. While they bring a subtle energy, they still have influence on our insights of day-to-day experiences and opportunities.

The transits of the personal planets happen regularly due to their faster orbits, bringing fairly frequent shifts in personal energy. These transits invite periods of reflection, preparation, and adjustment. For instance, Mercury retrograde can disrupt communication and technology (which is why we always back-up all online files before it begins), while Mars transits heighten ambition and drive, urging decisive actions. Because we know and expect these frequent transitions, we can make well-timed decisions, syncing our choices with the natural flow of cosmic energy.

## *Major Planetary Transits*

You may have guessed that the major transits involve the outer planets. These are the planets that extend beyond Earth and further into the galaxy and consist of all the planets from Jupiter to Pluto. Known as *generational planets*, they take longer to orbit the sun, and transits generally only occur a few times in our lives. Transits of outer planets may occur less frequently, but their effects have great impact over longer periods of time. Saturn, for example, stays in each sign for about two and a half years, bringing important lessons about responsibility and discipline. Uranus, on the other hand, spends around seven years in each sign, sparking radical shifts and self-reinvention. These slow and significant transits with their transformative energies can guide us through major life changes.

### *Relative Transit Positions and Their Effect*

Chapter 4 explained aspects (angles), and while each planet has a different effect, it's difficult to say which has a stronger influence. It would depend on the planetary positions of your birth chart to see which transits would affect you more.

#### Sun

When the transiting sun aligns with your birth sun, it highlights personal traits and achievements. Because the sun moves about one degree per day, its transits last roughly a week, but their influence can be significant. As the ruler of ego and self-expression, solar transits are a prime time for self-reflection or personal growth.

- Favorable aspects, such as trines, sextiles, and conjunctions offer support and energy, boost confidence, visibility, and leadership potential.

- Challenging aspects such as squares and oppositions may feel draining or confrontational and may bring power struggles, self-doubt, or excessive need for validation.

Solar transits often reveal what's most important to us and influence how we present ourselves to the world.

**Lunar**

These are the shortest transits, lasting only 2-3 days as the moon shifts signs. However, we know that even the briefest moments can impact our lives. The moon influences our emotions and desires, amplifying our feelings based on the planet's aspects.

For example, when the moon trines Pluto, it sharpens intuition and adds intensity to interactions.

- Positive aspects bring nurturing, bonding, and emotional expression.

- Challenging aspects may lead to moodiness, power struggles, and feelings of isolation.

A lunar transit can heighten sensitivity, soften harsher planetary effects, or deepen connections.

**Mercury**

When Mercury is transiting, our communication skills come into sharp focus. It's a time to either build connections or dismantle them. These transits spark innovation, helping us solve problems quickly or adjust how we manage daily routines. Mercury's fast pace gives a "seize the day" energy, with each transit lasting around 48-72 hours.

- Favorable transits inspire organization, quick learning, and stronger peer relationships.

- Challenging ones can lead to misunderstandings, schedule chaos, or decision overwhelm.

Mercury retrogrades offers us the chance to revisit these areas of our lives through a regularly repeating transit.

### Venus

Venus, the planet of love, beauty, and harmony, brings us a sense of romance and creativity during its transits. These movements are great for aesthetics, socializing, strengthening relationships, and making new connections.

- When Venus is in a harmonious aspect it softens energies, promoting attraction, and urges us to maintain the peace.
- Challenging aspects can reveal tension, indulgence, superficiality, and avoidance issues.

Venus transits encourage heart-opening experiences, self-expression, and a focus on beauty, but also demand authenticity to avoid falling into people-pleasing or shallow pursuits.

### Mars

Mars, the planet of action, stirs energy and drive during its transits, pushing us toward boldness and sometimes aggression. Mars amplifies determination and ambition, influencing our physical energy and romantic impulses.

- Igniting our personal or professional endeavors, Mars transits fuel desire and assertiveness.
- In challenging aspects, they may cause tension, recklessness, or heated interactions, making mindfulness and patience crucial.

These transits are prime moments for pursuing passions, starting projects, or tackling obstacles head-on but can also lead to rash decisions and conflicts.

### Jupiter

Jupiter's energy is all about expansion and amplification. During a Jupiter transit, which lasts for 1–2 months, confidence and optimism soar, but there's a risk of overindulging or overlooking important details.

- In favorable aspects, you may experience abundance, opportunities, breakthroughs, gain valuable advice and knowledge, or start new ventures. It's a great time to explore on both a personal and a professional level.

- Challenging aspects may magnify existing issues, encourage pointless pursuits, and a lack of diplomacy could cause conflict.

Jupiter's influence lasts longer due to its slow movement and yearly retrogrades, giving time for both its opportunities and challenges to unfold. Using Jupiter's expansive energy wisely can lead to growth.

### Saturn

Saturn, the planet of discipline, transits are slow and steady, lasting several months and recurs during its annual retrograde. It may close doors, slow progress, or bring challenges, but it pushes us to create practical solutions and long-term plans.

- When favorably positioned, Saturn helps us implement effective structures, take on leadership roles, strengthen healthy habits, or simplify our lives.

- In challenging aspects, it demands improvement in relationships and can bring tough lessons, delays, overwhelming tasks, and conflicts with authority.

Saturn acts as a tough but wise teacher, exposing weak spots in our lives and urging us to mature through hard work and persistence, ultimately rewarding patience and effort with lasting success.

**Uranus**

Uranus transits last 5-6 months and repeat over 2-3 years because of retrogrades. These are like electrifying shockwaves that disrupt our routine lives and push us toward radical change.

Uranus is associated with the unpredictable and is known to shake things up.

- If Uranus forms favorable aspects in our chart, it can bring moments of genius, new ideas, and connections with visionaries. We may find ourself more open to embracing individuality, joining liberal or progressive causes, and exploring unusual interests.

- When in challenging aspects, it may steer you toward rebellious actions, breaking away from stability, getting involved with the wrong crowd, or struggling with authority.

It encourages us to think outside the box and break free from the conventional. It's a time of impulsive decisions, rebellious energy, and revolutionary ideas, often linked to technology, innovation, and non-conformity.

**Neptune**

Neptune moves slowly, covering only five degrees per year. Its transits last for five months, repeating over several years due to its retrograde action. Neptune's influence lasts for 2–3 years, dissolving boundaries and revealing the need for stronger ones. Associated with the ethereal, it brings a haze of illusions and creativity, enhancing our imagination and intuition.

However, it also tempts us to escape reality, sometimes through addictive behaviors or fantasies, making it hard to stay grounded.

- In favorable aspects, Neptune encourages creative expression, healing, and spiritual growth. You may find it easier to connect with spiritual guides, angelic support, explore metaphysical practices, and trust the universe.

- In challenging aspects, it can result in confusion, addiction, codependency. We may become more vulnerable to toxicity, deception, and emotional exhaustion.

Maintaining healthy boundaries is key to navigating Neptune's dreamy, yet deceptive, energy

**Pluto**

Pluto moves slowly, covering only a few degrees each year, with its five-month retrograde causing repeated revisits to the same issues. Pluto transits, lasting 3–5 years are often intensely disruptive. Pluto brings hidden desires, power struggles, and deep-seated emotions to the surface. It forces us to confront what's been simmering beneath, leading to powerful transformation that may feel unavoidable. It's a process that can take place over several years, as Pluto highlights areas of power, rebirth, and uncovering hidden truths.

- In favorable aspects, Pluto supports changes for the better and helps us step into our power, rise from setbacks, and undergo deep emotional healing. It's not unusual to find ourselves exploring the mystical or start developing psychic abilities.

- Challenging aspects may trigger power struggles, betrayal, jealousy, or obsessive behavior. You may face loss, confront the hidden, or feel overpowered by darker urges.

Pluto's energy, though intense, ultimately leads to personal growth through necessary destruction and renewal.

## Progressions

Planetary progressions involve the gradual movement of planets through our birth chart that highlight shifts in energy and focus in different areas of our lives. As the planets progress, they influence personal development and life experiences. For instance, a progressing Saturn could bring lessons, through challenges, about responsibility.

A progressing Venus may enhance relationships and creativity. These changes can affect either our inner or outer worlds depending on the position of other celestial bodies in relation to the progressing planet.

This movement through the various sun signs and houses could potentially affect you by manifesting as opportunities, challenges, and significant changes. Each birth chart has its own unique qualities and energies, determining how we experience love, career, health, and personal growth.

## *Progressed charts*

A progressed chart is a valuable predictive tool in astrology that illustrates the evolution of our natal chart as we age. This chart is created by advancing the natal chart forward, with each day following birth symbolizing one year of life.

- Identify the date for progression for age 20: If you were born on February 18, 1981, your progression chart at age 20 would be calculated based on the planetary positions 20 days after your birth.
    - February 18, 1981 + 20 days = March 10, 1981.
    - The positions of the planets, ascendant, and midheaven on March 10, 1981, will represent your progressed chart when you are 20 years old in 2001.
- Identify the date for progression for age 30: To find your progressed chart at the age of 30, add 30 days to your birth date.
    - February 18, 1981 + 30 days = March 20, 1981.
    - The positions of the planets on March 20, 1981, represent your progressed chart for age 30 (the year 2011).

- Identify the date for progression for age 50: To find your progressed chart at the age of 50, you need to add 50 days to your birth date.
    - February 18, 1981 + 50 days = April 9, 1981.
    - The planetary positions on April 9, 1981, represent your progressed chart for age 50 (the year 2031).

By utilizing this chart, you can gain insight into your personal development and identify pathways to fulfill their potential. This is a powerful tool for self-discovery and introspection, helping you to understand the direction your life has or is taking and the influences that may shape it.

I came across a lovely explanation of how this works (The Astro Twins, n.d.). Imagine that, like your phone, you arrive fresh in this world with predetermined factory settings. Every few months, years, or even decades, you, or certain areas of your life (like your installed apps), need an upgrade. Sometimes, these are improvements, and sometimes there are glitches and system issues, but each update or upgrade is designed to help you grow and improve your life experience.

## *The Difference Between Progressed Charts and Transit Charts*

Progressed charts reveal gradual, long-term personal evolution, making their influence more profound and longer-lasting than standard transit charts.

If a planet was retrograde at birth, it could remain retrograde for years in the progressed chart. Progressed aspects last longer than transits, with the moon's aspects active for months, and those of the sun, Venus, Mars, and Mercury extending for years.

Jupiter and Saturn are considered "middle planets," moving at moderate speeds in both transit and progressed charts. They rarely change signs in a progressed chart during a lifetime, unless positioned at the sign's final degrees at birth. Jupiter moves one degree every 12 years, and Saturn, every 18 years. A sign or directional change for either planet in the progressed chart signals a significant shift or life phase.

## *Progressed Charts and Decision-Making*

Progressed charts are among the most insightful resources in astrology, revealing the gradual shifts in personality and emotional development throughout your life. By exploring these changes, you can gain a deeper understanding of your life's evolution and the maturation of your soul. This knowledge enables you to anticipate transitions and navigate challenges with greater ease.

Progressed charts bring you closer to understanding your journey while allowing you to embrace the mysteries that life presents. When consulting an astrologer before major decisions, they will consult your birth chart as well as one or both of a transit or progression chart.

### *Career Opportunities*

- **Midheaven (MC)**: The midheaven signifies your public persona, life direction, and how you're perceived in the world, often reflecting your professional path and achievements. The sign on the midheaven and any nearby planets provide insight into your potential career trajectory and approach to success.

- **Saturn**: Saturn is closely linked to the effort and perseverance needed to build a lasting career. The placement of Saturn, by sign and house, reveals where you focus your efforts, face challenges, and develop professional stability over time.

- **Sun**: Although not generally a career indicator, the sun points to work that aligns with your purpose and brings you fulfillment. The sun's position sheds light on career paths that resonate with your identity and values.

- **Jupiter**: Jupiter can reveal where you may encounter opportunities for advancement, success, and recognition in your career. Jupiter's sign and house placement suggest areas where you naturally thrive and are rewarded for your efforts.

- **Venus**: Venus often influences careers related to art, design, luxury, or any field that requires a refined sense of aesthetics. Venus' placement shows your inclination toward professions that emphasize relationships, creativity, or the creation of value and harmony.

- **Mercury**: Mercury plays a significant role in careers that involve writing, teaching, technology, or commerce. The placement of Mercury provides clues about your communication style and how you apply your intellectual abilities in professional settings.

- **Mars**: Mars shows how you approach your career goals and handle professional challenges. The sign and house position of Mars reveal where you direct your energy and the type of work that excites and drives you forward.

- **North Node**: The North Node symbolizes your life's purpose and growth potential. It offers insight into the broader direction or calling you're meant to pursue, often pointing toward the career path that will lead to personal and spiritual development.

Beyond these planetary influences, the 6th House (daily work and service) and the 2nd House (finances and resources) are also essential in determining and refining career matters, offering additional insight related to work and success.

### *Finance*

- **Jupiter**: Jupiter is often regarded as the most important planet when it comes to wealth accumulation. It represents expansion, wisdom, and prosperity, offering opportunities for financial success. A strong Jupiter in the horoscope indicates that an individual is likely to experience growth in wealth, often through wise investments, business ventures, or fortunate circumstances. Jupiter ensures that wealth is acquired in an ethical and sustainable way, contributing to long-term financial security.

- **Venus**: Venus governs luxury, comfort, and material abundance. It is associated with financial gains through artistic, creative, and aesthetic pursuits, including partnerships and business investments. A strong Venus in one's birth chart can bring financial success, particularly through ventures that involve beauty, creativity, or relationships. Venus also signifies wealth that allows for a life filled with luxury and high-end comforts.

- **Mercury**: Mercury is crucial for financial success in business and commerce. It governs communication, trade, and intellectual pursuits, influencing out ability to make smart financial decisions. A well-placed Mercury enhances business acumen and facilitates successful financial transactions. Whether through strategic investments, business negotiations, or intellectual endeavors, Mercury's influence can significantly boost wealth accumulation.

- **Moon**: The moon plays an essential role in emotional well-being, which directly impacts financial stability. It governs your ability to save and accumulate wealth over time. A strong and well-placed moon indicates financial security, allowing for stability and growth in your financial life. Emotional clarity and good judgment, influenced by the moon, contribute to sound financial decisions.

In addition to the planetary influences, the 2nd House (wealth and finance) governs personal assets, money, and overall financial status. A strong 2nd House, supported by favorable planets, indicates significant wealth accumulation and financial security.

The 11th House (income) represents financial gains and opportunities for increasing wealth.

- **Moon**: The moon reveals how you process emotions and respond to life's challenges. It represents your true self beneath the surface. In relationships, understanding your moon sign is crucial, as it helps ensure your partner resonates with how you handle emotions and conflict. Ideally, having a partner who processes feelings similarly to you fosters a deeper emotional understanding and harmony.

- **Mercury**: Mercury shapes your communication style. Finding someone who communicates in a way that complements yours can reduce misunderstandings and enhance clarity in the relationship. When partners align in their communication, expressing needs becomes easier and leaving little room for confusion.

- **Venus**: Venus reveals how you give and receive love, showing your romantic style and what makes you feel cherished. It governs your love language, indicating what you need from a partner to feel valued in a relationship, how you like to be pursued, and the way you show affection in return.

- **Mars**: Mars speaks to your sexual energy and how you assert yourself in a partnership. Sexual compatibility is vital for lasting attraction, and a strong Mars connection between partners ensures a natural, enduring physical chemistry that keeps the relationship vibrant over time.

There are a number of houses that need to be consulted when it comes to love and relationships.

- The 5th House reveals what you enjoy in your leisure time and the traits you find attractive in a romantic partner. It also highlights the type of activities that bring you joy, both individually and with a lover.

- The 7th House governs long-term relationships, including marriage. It shows what qualities you seek in a committed partner and what you're willing to commit to in a relationship.

- The 8th House focuses on deep intimacy and sexual compatibility. It represents the type of partner who will connect with you on a profound, physical level, ensuring strong chemistry in the bedroom.

- The 11th House governs friendships and social circles. People with traits related to this house tend to form close, lasting friendships with you easily, enhancing the companionship aspect of any relationship.

### *Personal Transformation*

- **Mercury**: Mercury shapes the way we think, process information, and engage with others so that we sharpen our ability to convey ideas clearly and understand our thought patterns. Mercury offers spiritual lessons in mindful communication and clarity of thought, guiding us to connect with higher wisdom and improve our mental awareness.

- **Venus**: Venus teaches the importance of cultivating self-love and establishing healthy boundaries. Spiritually, Venus encourages us to seek inner balance and compassion, inspiring love in all areas of life and helping us align with the divine essence of beauty and connection.

- **Mars**: Mars guides us in channeling our energy into disciplined action, helping us stay focused and persistent. Spiritually, Mars awakens the inner warrior, urging us to act with integrity and align our actions with our higher purpose, reminding us of the power of will in manifesting our dreams.

- **Jupiter and Saturn**: Jupiter and Saturn offer complementary energies that balance growth and discipline. Jupiter represents optimism, expansion, and opportunities, fostering spiritual growth by broadening our horizons and deepening our connection to higher beliefs. Saturn, on the other hand, brings structure, responsibility, and the lessons of limitation, teaching us the value of patience, perseverance, and inner-strength on both personal and spiritual levels. Together, they encourage us to grow while staying grounded.

The first six houses are all involved in our personal development and those things that are closest to our hearts. As you progress through these houses, you move from personal identity to self-expression and then grow toward service.

- First House defines beginnings, your identity, and how you present yourself to the world. It represents your sense of self and initiates personal development.

- Second House is tied to values, self-esteem, income, and material resources, helping you build confidence and security in both body and environment.

- Third House governs all forms of communication, which is a key factor of our personal growth and emotional intelligence.

- Fourth House influences how you nurture yourself and others, shaping your emotional foundation.

- Fifth House reveals how you engage in artistic pursuits and celebrate life.

- Sixth House covers daily routines, health, and service, and practical matters, encouraging organization, well-being, and the desire to serve others and the planet.

### *Communication and Learning*

- Mercury: The planet of communication governs how we convey our thoughts and ideas, influencing everything from speech to writing. Those with a strong Mercury influence often display eloquence, mental agility, and adaptability in conversation. During Mercury retrograde, however, communication can become more challenging, leading to misinterpretations, delays, or confusion.

- Venus: Venus lends a touch of charm, grace, and tact to conversations. People under Venus' influence tend to prioritize harmonious interactions, using diplomacy to ensure smooth and pleasant exchanges. They strive to create warmth and connection in their communication.

- Jupiter: Jupiter amplifies communication with optimism, enthusiasm, and a love for big ideas. It encourages broad-minded, philosophical discussions filled with inspiration and storytelling. Those guided by Jupiter often seek to uplift and share knowledge through their conversations.

- Saturn: Saturn brings structure, responsibility, and a focus on clarity in communication. Those influenced by Saturn are methodical and thoughtful, preferring disciplined, accurate, and well-considered speech.

The 3rd House in astrology governs all forms of communication, from writing and speaking to editing and research. The 3rd House influences teaching, public speaking, and journalism, and it emphasizes facts, negotiation, and the handling of agreements and contracts. It's a house grounded in information gathering and the exchange of knowledge, shaping the way we interact with the world through communication.

### *Home and Family*

- **Jupiter**: Jupiter is often linked to family in astrology. It represents the values we cherish, including our loved ones, home, and community. Beyond material wealth, Jupiter is also tied to tradition and authority, playing a significant role in shaping the core beliefs and family values passed down through generations.

- **Venus**: As the planet of love, beauty, and harmony, Venus influences the emotional ties within the family. It governs the bonds between family members, contributing to the warmth and affection that define family life. Additionally, Venus can reflect the aesthetic and physical aspects that make a home feel inviting and peaceful.

- **Moon**: The moon rules over emotions, nurturing, and the concept of home, often symbolizing the maternal figure. It represents our emotional needs and attachments, shaping our connection with family members and the security we find in the family unit.

- **Sun**: The sun plays a pivotal role in the family dynamic. It reflects the patriarch or authority within the family structure but also our own personal identity and the role we take on within the family.

The 4th House speaks to our roots, early upbringing, and our relationships with parents and close relatives. It highlights our sense of security and the foundational experiences that shape our family identity. The 10th House focuses on the paternal role within the family.

### *Health and Vitality*

All of the inner celestial bodies (personal planets) have a role to play when it comes to health and wellness. So too do the middle planets, Jupiter and Saturn. Each is associated with specific areas of the body.

- **Sun**: The sun represents vitality, governing our overall physical constitution, with a focus on the heart, spine, and general health. A well-positioned sun can indicate strong immunity and high energy levels, while an ill-placed sun may suggest issues with heart health or low vitality.

- **Moon**: The moon governs bodily fluids, with influence over the stomach, breasts, and menstrual cycle. A strong moon brings emotional stability and good digestion, whereas a weak moon can lead to emotional imbalance and digestive problems.

- **Mars**: Mars rules over the muscles, blood, and immune system. A well-aspected Mars enhances physical stamina and immunity, while a challenged Mars might lead to inflammatory conditions or injuries.

- **Mercury**: Mercury controls the nervous system, while also influencing the respiratory system, skin, and nerves. A favorable Mercury sharpens intellect and bolsters communication, while an unfavorable Mercury may result in nervous system disorders or skin problems.

- **Jupiter**: Jupiter governs the liver, pancreas, and fat regulation. A strong Jupiter supports a healthy metabolism and good liver function, while a weak Jupiter may bring about issues such as liver dysfunction or obesity.

- **Venus**: Venus rules the reproductive organs, kidneys, and skin. A well-placed Venus supports clear skin and healthy reproductive function, whereas a poorly positioned Venus may lead to kidney or skin problems.

- **Saturn**: Saturn is tied chronic conditions, governing bones, teeth, and joints. A positive Saturn placement fosters endurance and strong bones, while a weak Saturn can result in joint issues or chronic ailments.

The 1st House represents the body's constitution, general health, and vitality. It influences the head and face. The 6th House governs overall health, particularly the digestive system and intestines.

## Planetary Hours

Before diving into the concept of planetary days, it's essential to grasp the foundation behind this ancient system. Planetary days connect each day of the week with one of the celestial bodies in our solar system, and each brings its unique influence to the day or night they are associated with.

What that means is that each day is infused with the energy of its planet, making certain days more suitable for taking certain actions than others.

1. Monday is associated with the moon's day (Latin—*Lunae*)
2. Tuesday is associated with day of Mars (Latin—*Martis*)
3. Wednesday with the day of Mercury (Latin—*Mercurii*)
4. Thursday with the day of Jupiter (Latin—*Lovis*)
5. Friday with the day of Venus (Latin—*Veneris*)
6. Saturday with the day of Saturn (Latin—*Saturni*)
7. Sunday with the sun's day (Latin—*Solis*)

Planetary hours follow the Chaldean order, an ancient system that arranges the seven traditional planets according to their speed. The first hour of any day, which starts at sunrise, is ruled by the planet associated with that day. For instance, on Monday, the first hour after sunrise is always the moon hour. The sequence then continues as follows: Saturn, Jupiter, Mars, sun, Venus, Mercury, and moon.

This pattern repeats 12 times throughout the day starting at sunrise and ending at sunset. The Chaldean order, based on the average speed of the planets, starts with Saturn, the slowest, and ends with the moon, the fastest. As you move through the sequence, you're transitioning from the planet with the slowest velocity to the quickest.

It's important to note that the length of planetary hours varies based on location. Due to the Earth's tilt, days aren't exactly 24 hours long, and planetary hours don't always last 60 minutes. The duration of each hour depends on your position in relation to the equator.

You can calculate the exact length of a planetary hour by dividing the time between sunrise and sunset into 12 equal parts and adjusting for local conditions.

How to calculate planetary hours:

Sunrise: 5:14 am

Sunset: 18:21 (6:21 pm)

Step 1. Find total daylight hours:

- 18:21 - 5:14 = 13 hours and 7 minutes of daylight.

Step 2. Convert length of daytime into minutes:

- 13 hours = 780 minutes
- 7 minutes = 7 minutes

Total daylight time is:

- 780 + 7 = 787 minutes

Step 3. Divide by 12 for the length of each planetary hour:

- 787 ÷ 12 = 65.58 minutes

Each planetary daytime hour is approximately 65.6 minutes (or around 65 minutes and 35 seconds).

You can then use the planetary hours for manifestation:

**Sun Hour**

- Manifest: Success, recognition, inspiration
- Actions: Launch important initiatives, set goals for maximum impact

**Venus Hour**

- Manifest: Love, beauty, peace

- Actions: Go on a date, pamper yourself, or dive into artistic ventures

**Mercury Hour**

- Manifest: Sharpen the mind, communicate ideas, foster travel safety
- Actions: Plan projects, learn something new, socialize, or work on writing tasks

**Moon Hour**

- Manifest: Family building, emotional healing, nurturing
- Actions: Meditate, journal, or connect with a counselor

**Saturn Hour**

- Manifest: Release, discipline, constructing new habits
- Actions: Focus on long-term goals, let go of toxic patterns

**Jupiter Hour**

- Manifest: Prosperity, luck, opportunities
- Actions: Sign important documents, ask for help, explore new opportunities

**Mars Hour**

- Manifest: Victory, increased passion, competitiveness
- Actions: Exercise, engage in sports, or revitalize relationships

Although planetary hours traditionally involve the seven classical planets, modern astrology offers ways to work with the energies of Uranus, Neptune, and Pluto. These outer planets, discovered later, are considered *higher octaves* of their corresponding inner planets.

Uranus is associated with Mercury for its influence on intellect and innovation.

Neptune resonates with Venus and its connection to love and creativity.

Pluto is connected to Mars with its emphasis on action and power.

## *A Note on Planetary Nights*

Just as each planetary day begins with a specific planetary hour at sunrise—Monday starts with moon hour, Tuesday with Mars hour—planetary nights function similarly by starting with the corresponding planetary hour at sunset.

What this means is that sunset starts at the 13th planetary day hour, or rather the first planetary night hour; they're one and the same. Consider Friday, ruled by Venus. The day begins at sunrise with Venus hour. Thirteen "hours" later would be occupied by Mars, so Mars would be the first "hour" of the night. This continues until the next sunset which will fall on Saturn's day. Therefore, each night would fall as indicated below.

Monday: Venus night

Tuesday: Saturn night

Wednesday: Sun night

Thursday: Moon night

Friday: Mars night

Saturday: Mercury night

Sunday: Jupiter night

The idea behind planetary nights might seem complex because we're not used to thinking that way, and like anything unfamiliar, it's simply a matter of getting used to a new idea.

## Lunar Cycles

The phases of the moon represent different stages in its journey, each holding unique significance.

- **New Moon**: A new moon occurs when the moon is directly between the sun and Earth and the dark side of the moon faces Earth, making it difficult to see.
    - Action: Reflect, look within, plan, and allow your intuition to guide you.
- **Waxing Crescent Moon**: As the moon moves from its position between Earth and the sun, it gradually becomes lighter over the next few days. This appears as a crescent and gets larger each day.
    - Action: Initiate change, new beginnings, set goals, and self-improvement.
- **First Quarter Moon**: This phase is when half of the moon facing Earth is illuminated and challenges may appear to come to light.
    - Action: Make decisive decisions and work on removing obstacles or overcoming difficulties.
- **Waxing Gibbous Moon**: Appearing as a very full crescent and occurring just before the full moon, most of the moon is lit and is often visible during daylight.
    - Action: Identify what hasn't been working in your favor and make adjustments.

- **Full Moon**: When the sun and moon are on opposite sides of Earth, the sun can light up the whole side of the moon that's facing Earth and is also often visible during the day.
    - Action: Celebrate successes. Things brought to light need to be examined.
- **Waning Gibbous**: The moon begins to move in front of the sun once again and a full crescent appears. This is on the opposite side of the waxing gibbous moon.
    - Action: Express gratitude and realign and adjust your intentions where necessary.
- **Third Quarter Moon**: Also called the *last quarter moon*, it appears as a half-moon, opposite to the side of the first quarter moon.
    - Action: Release. Let go of what doesn't serve you and cleanse your surroundings and your energy.
- **Waning Crescent Moon**: The moon is once more a sliver of light as it prepares to enter the new moon phase.
    - Action: Release everything to the universe. Rest. Reconnect. This is a perfect time for a spa day.

Did you know that the side of the crescents appear differently in each hemisphere? In its waxing phase, the crescent appears on the right side of the moon from the northern hemisphere and is on the left side if you're in the southern hemisphere.

## Mercury and Decision-Making

Mercury holds a special place in shaping decision-making skills, often seen as the planet that governs intellect, communication, and reasoning. When Mercury's influence is strong in your life, it brings a host of benefits, including sharper thinking, clearer communication, and a boost in your mental agility.

## *Mercury's Influence on Success*

A strong Mercury enhances your ability to learn, retain knowledge, and articulate your thoughts with clarity and confidence. It helps you express ideas in a way that resonates with others. For those with writing aspirations, Mercury's energy can refine your ability to craft words, making you a more compelling storyteller or communicator.

It also boosts your decision-making abilities by honing your analytical mind, logic, and reasoning. Under its influence, you can make choices rooted in objectivity and rationality, relying on facts rather than emotions, leading to better decisions.

Mercury is also connected to commerce, finance, and business, opening the door to financial prosperity by sharpening your aptitude for financial planning, accounting, and investments. Whether you're starting a business or managing your personal finances, Mercury's influence can help you strategize effectively and spot opportunities that others might miss.

## *Mercury and Finding Your Voice*

Beyond sharpening logic and intellect, Mercury also governs self-expression. Your voice is not limited to what you say or write; it's the embodiment of your inner world, emotions, and personal power. Your voice can stutter with uncertainty, flirt with excitement, or tremble with vulnerability.

It's a complex mix of your experiences, emotions, and inner thoughts. Finding your voice, especially if you've felt unheard in the past, is essential to unlocking your full potential. Mercury's energy can help you harness your true voice, not just in words but in how you carry your ideas and express your power creatively and authentically.

### *Making Decisions*

When a decision needs to be made, it would be best to consult a professional astrologer until you're comfortable with astrology. An alternative is to check online at planetarium or astronomy sites. They can tell you everything about where the different celestial bodies are in the sky at all times. These usually include moon phases, asteroids, and comets too.

When getting this information, consider any occurring transits, your progression chart, where the planets are in relation to the houses, as well as any astrological predictions for the coming days, weeks, or months. Where possible, align with the planetary days and nights, and where you can, the planetary hours.

Take into account that we are all raised uniquely and the influence of our family, society, and culture will affect the way we view ourselves and the world.

Lastly, we are all born with a sense of intuition. Your intuition may come across as a voice whispering in your ear, a gut feeling, or simply a sense that you can't quite put your finger on. Always, always listen to your intuition. It seldom leads you in the wrong direction.

How many times have you heard of something happening, like a plane crash, and certain people who were booked on it never boarded the plane? Their intuition was usually responsible.

So, if your horoscope says that it's a good day to go hiking and your gut says "no," listen to your gut rather than your peers or worry about money wasted.

Following the combined guidance of all the above, as long as you don't behave irresponsibly, will lead you to the best-case scenario, or at the very least, provide a lesson that you are ready to learn.

# Progression Quiz

1. **What is the significance of planetary transits in astrology?**

    a. They show the current weather patterns.

    b. They predict person's daily routines.

    c. They represent the movement of planets and their impact on individuals.

    d. They signify the age of a person.

2. **How are progressed charts used in decision-making, according to astrology?**

    a. They are used to decide the best time for business investments.

    b. They are used to analyze a person's development over time.

    c. They are used to predict natural disasters.

    d. They have no significance in decision-making.

3. **In terms of career opportunities, which planet plays a significant role, according to astrology?**

    a. Mars

    b. Venus

    c. Jupiter

    d. Mercury

4. **What does Mercury's role in decision-making involve?**

    a. It influences communication and learning abilities.

b. It controls emotional stability.

c. It governs physical strength and health.

d. It decides wealth accumulation.

**5. What is the purpose of studying lunar cycles in astrology?**

a. To predict future events based on moon phases.

b. To understand agricultural patterns.

c. To study its effect on ocean tides.

d. None of the above.

## *Answers*

1. c. They represent the movement of planets and their impact on individuals.
2. b. They are used to analyze a person's development over time.
3. d. Mercury
4. a. It influences communication and learning abilities.
5. a. To predict future events based on moon phases.

Chapter 7:

# Stress Relief and Wellness

Stress is an unavoidable fact of life, but the way we are affected by stress depends on the type of stress and the way we deal with it. The fast-paced world we live in often blinds us to the sources of our stress and sometimes, we make decisions without thinking them through which only increases our stress levels.

Whether they come from professional demands, relationship issues, or our personal thoughts, dreams, and concerns, the stress we experience often lies beneath the surface of our awareness.

Stress interferes with both our mental and physical well-being.

By examining planetary alignments, astrology offers us clues into the underlying causes of our stress. By recognizing these influences, we are provided both direction and the tools to manage our stress effectively.

## Chiron and Our Core Unconscious Stressors

In Greek mythology, Chiron was a wise centaur who could heal others but was unable to heal his own wounds. Known as the *wounded healer* in mythology, Chiron holds significant astrological meaning. Despite being a minor planet, Chiron's position in your birth chart reveals where your deepest wounds lie and highlights recurring life challenges. These refer to pain that has been inflicted on you rather than through your errors in judgement. In astrology, Chiron symbolizes the journey from suffering to wisdom. Its placement in your chart uncovers areas of vulnerability, personal healing, and transformation.

When we become aware of our vulnerabilities, we can harness our wisdom, experience, and strengths to transform that pain into a source of healing, helping us move beyond emotional scars.

Although it is human nature to want to suppress or avoid our pain, Chiron's placement urges us to face it head-on. Only by acknowledging our painful experiences, can we transform our challenges into opportunities for growth. It frees us from being blocked by our pain. This process can be empowering and reveal hidden potential. In doing so, we turn our suffering into something positive as we are guided toward that potential. However, transforming pain into wisdom requires courage, self-reflection, and intentional action. Suggested ways to do this include looking within through actions such as journaling, therapy, dream recall, inner child work, writing letters to your younger self, or using positive affirmations.

- Chiron in Aries (1st House): You may experience feelings of isolation, which can manifest as anger, aloofness, or a competitive nature.

- Chiron in Taurus (2nd House): Resistance to change, addictive tendencies, and financial struggles could be central themes for you.
- Chiron in Gemini (3rd House): You might fear loneliness and judgment, potentially using gossip as a way to connect with others.
- Chiron in Cancer (4th House): Struggles with feeling safe in the world and unresolved issues related to your mother may be prominent.
- Chiron in Leo (5th House): You could attract drama and have a strong need for validation and attention from others.
- Chiron in Virgo (6th House): Perfectionism, self-criticism, hypersensitivity to criticism, and concerns about health might be recurring challenges.
- Chiron in Libra (7th House): You may face difficulties with relationships, commitment issues, or a tendency to romanticize partnerships.
- Chiron in Scorpio (8th House): Struggles with jealousy and obsessive tendencies could be significant for you.
- Chiron in Sagittarius (9th House): You might constantly seek new thrills or exhibit aggression in your communication style.
- Chiron in Capricorn (10th House): Ambition could become an obsession, and you may grapple with unresolved issues related to your father.
- Chiron in Aquarius (11th House): You may struggle with rebellion and feel like an outsider, never quite fitting in.
- Chiron in Pisces (12th House): Boundaries may be difficult for you to establish, and you might retreat into fantasy rather than face reality.

The Chiron return, which typically occurs around the age of 50, marks the celestial body's completion of its cycle through the astrological birth chart. This significant event often triggers a deeper level of self-awareness and healing. It offers a chance to revisit old wounds, seek resolution, and find lasting inner peace, allowing you to reassess your life's purpose with renewed clarity and understanding.

## Moon Signs and Understanding Our Emotional Nature

You already understand that your moon sign may not be as outwardly visible as your sun sign, but it plays a crucial role in shaping your emotional world and inner depths. It governs your moods and can often explain why you might feel misunderstood. In cases where a confident Leo sun is paired with a sensitive Pisces moon, there is likely to be a mix of external strength and inner vulnerability. By embracing the differences between your sun and moon signs, you can better understand your emotional needs and develop a deeper sense of self-compassion and balance.

### *Coping Mechanisms Based on Moon Signs*

We are all unique, and while we may share similarities when something or someone pulls at our heartstrings or fires us up in indignation, when it comes to the way we handle our personal business, our moon signs can shed some light on our behavior. Here we examine the traits of each moon sign, followed by the challenges and finally, a suggested solution.

#### Moon in Aries

Make yourself and your emotions a top priority. Lean into your go-getter spirit, but be mindful of the need to release pent-up energy, particularly when frustrated or impatient. Embrace serenity. Meditation can help temper impulsive reactions and soothe fiery emotions, grounding your vibrant energy.

**Moon in Taurus**

You naturally gravitate toward comfort and sensory pleasure. Drawn to routine, you may be resistant to change. Embrace your love for the sensual by pampering yourself; cook a wholesome meal, slip into something luxurious, and treat yourself, whether it's a gourmet dinner, a night out, or a serene escape into nature. With your sensual nature, you'll feel revitalized by long baths, showers, or even a well-deserved spa day.

**Moon in Gemini**

Your quick wit and love for conversation drive your emotional expression. Your constantly buzzing mind can sometimes get in the way of processing deeper feelings. Dive into mentally stimulating outlets like journaling, reading, or creating art. Connect with friends for meaningful conversations and explore just for fun. Since communication is your emotional compass, it's essential for you to truly understand and work through your feelings.

**Moon in Cancer**

Your emotions run deep, and you find comfort in the sanctuary of home. It's important to prioritize self-care so that your sense of worth isn't only tied to caring for others. To replenish your energy, create a cozy, personal grounding space. Tap into your inner child by enjoying nostalgic activities and give yourself time to rest, release emotions, and practice self-compassion.

**Moon in Leo**

Your creativity shines brightly through expressive outlets like drawing, dancing, or embracing moments of playfulness. When emotions run high, don't shy away from a little drama; share your story theatrically with a friend to release those feelings. Afterward, shift your focus to practical problem-solving. Your gift is generosity, so channel it by nurturing both yourself and those around you.

### Moon in Virgo

Stability comes from having control, which can make adapting to changes feel difficult. You excel when you focus on mindful habits, such as intentional movement and balanced nutrition. It's important to take time to focus on yourself, so find ways to prioritize your needs, whether by assigning tasks to others or using AI tools to streamline your responsibilities. Give your mind a break with activities like watching TV, enjoying crafts, or listening to audiobooks, all of which can help alleviate stress and keep anxiety at bay.

### Moon in Libra

Your aversion to conflict and extremes may cause hesitation or a tendency to prioritize others' needs over your own. Communicating your desires clearly and embracing self-love is important for your inner peace. Surround yourself with beauty and nurturing self-care routines like a spa day at home. Create moments of stillness in environments that bring you joy.

### Moon in Scorpio

You feel emotions with great intensity but hide them beneath the surface. When you struggle to express your emotions, you can retreat into secrecy as a form of self-protection. Pour your intensity into creating transformative and healing spaces. When alone, smudge and engage in rituals of emotional release or sensual self-care to clear stagnant energy. Imagine both the worst and best possible outcomes and step into your renewed, empowered self. Release past wounds through forgiveness rituals, such as writing down feelings and tearing them up, symbolizing your freedom from past baggage.

### Moon in Sagittarius

You feel most alive in nature, learning new things, and sharing experiences with those who share your thirst for discovery. It's essential to honor your need for freedom and adventure but also to face situations that challenge you without running away. Channel your fiery energy by embracing outdoor pursuits, or satisfy your curiosity through learning while you unwind. Work on staying grounded in nature's energy. Find inspiration in tales of exploration and hold onto your sense of independence, even within your closest relationships.

### Moon in Capricorn

Make sure to carve out time for rest and joy without sacrificing your sense of productivity. Use a planner to manage both work tasks and personal care; scheduling something like a massage can help you release built-up tension. Ground yourself and remember to take time to laugh and embrace the lighter side of life. Set healthy boundaries, don't hesitate to ask for help, and allow others to support and care for you when you need it.

### Moon in Aquarius

Without direction, you might find yourself rebelling aimlessly, and in your quest to rise above your emotions, you could inadvertently isolate yourself from those around you. You flourish when actively contributing to society, valuing your independence, and surrounding yourself with friends who honor that need. Consider supporting a cause that resonates with you or delving into energy healing practices. It's important that you stay authentic at all times.

### Moon in Pisces

You may find it challenging to articulate your emotions, and your heightened sensitivity can sometimes drive you toward escapism.

Concentrate on setting emotional boundaries and indulge in solitary self-care rituals. Try incorporating water-based cleansing practices, such as soothing baths with seaweed and sea salt, and allow your creativity to flourish through artistic pursuits and divination.

Give yourself permission to engage in activities that come naturally and explore your imagination fully. Embrace your intuitive and creative side through dance, photography, or writing; let your expression be uniquely yours.

## Stress Relief Tips Based on Sun Signs

Each sun sign has its own challenges and ways of dealing with stress and wellness. Remember that your emotions affect your mind, and these have a knock-on effect on your physical health.

**Aries**: Hit the gym! Working out is the best way to ground and get rid of any negative energy; both your body and mind will thank you for it!

**Taurus**: You love indulging, so watch what you eat and choose healthy options. Direct negative energy into finding ways to make healthy food taste delicious.

**Gemini**: Settle your intensely active mind by dissecting and analyzing facts and then check them again. But do so calmly. Feeling that you're being proactive will help settle you.

**Cancer**: Create a sanctuary for yourself at home, whether in a room or outdoors. When you need it, demand your space and your *me time.*

**Leo**: Get creative. With your bright personality and generosity, sharing a new idea or creation, or even showcasing it in your own space makes you feel good about yourself.

**Virgo**: The action of doing something physical, like cleaning, that is necessary and doesn't require much thought allows you to use the time for your mind to process what it needs to.

**Libra**: Speaking to someone close to you helps put any issues into perspective, providing clarity and putting your mind at ease.

**Scorpio**: Sexuality and fantasy are the best stress relieving methods for you. If one is not available, then you have an alternate or combined option.

**Sagittarius**: You love inspirational stories, quotes, and philosophical gurus. Create a journal with your own philosophies. This will help you define your objectives, thus relieving anxiety.

**Capricorn**: When stressed, draw up a new game plan or look for ways to improve those your already have. Directing your mind toward actionable goals will ease your mind.

**Aquarius**: Start a vision board that depicts your ideal future or find a common goal with friends and have a group vision board with action steps that you all contribute to.

**Pisces**: Meditate and ground. As a natural empath, taking time out to step back into your own emotions and feelings is vital for your peace of mind and emotional calm.

## Daily Rituals Using the 6th House in the Natal Chart

The 6th House is associated with habits and health and knowing where your sun sign appears in this house can help combat stress and add to your general health. Below are suggestions for each sign.

**Aries**: Engage in intense physical activities, challenging sports, or martial arts competitions. Learn to be mindful and slow down momentarily.

**Taurus**: It's essential to connect with nature and create a comfortable workspace. Integrating beauty and sensuality into daily routines supports balance.

**Gemini**: Your social connections are crucial as long periods of isolation can be tough. Reading, journaling, or conversation can help recharge social energy.

**Cancer**: A comforting work environment is vital as is emotional awareness. Connecting with pets or engaging in moon phases can boost wellness.

**Leo**: Enjoy a playful approach to life, focusing on creativity and resilience. Volunteering with children brings joy, and creative outlets enhance daily rituals.

**Virgo**: It's important to manage perfectionism and adopt mindfulness practices. Grounding activities like gardening promote good health.

**Libra**: With strong mediating and counseling tendencies, boundaries need to be set to maintain energy levels. Leisure activities like yoga and aromatherapy are beneficial.

**Scorpio**: Incorporate daily pleasure practices and emotional release. Balance is crucial, participate in both serious and light-hearted activities.

**Sagittarius**: Ensure your freedom and flexibility in health and wellness routines. Set up personalized schedules and spiritual practices that align with your adventurous spirit.

**Capricorn**: A natural leader in wellness, you may overlook personal needs. Include strength training, but routines should incorporate rest and self-care.

**Aquarius**: Enjoy serving others, but limit news consumption to avoid overwhelm. Creative outlets and innovative health tools enhance well-being.

**Pisces**: Your strong intuitive abilities suggest the potential for a holistic wellness career. Vital to maintain awareness of emotional boundaries and engage in practices like dream journaling and energy cleansing for maintaining health.

## Progression Quiz

1. **What is the role of Chiron in astrology?**

    a. It represents our career path.

    b. It shows our core unconscious stressors.

    c. It decides our love life.

    d. It shows our financial prospects.

2. **How does understanding your moon sign contribute to stress relief and wellness?**

    a. It helps you choose your friends wisely.

    b. It aids in understanding your emotional nature and reactions.

    c. It guides you on what foods to eat for better health.

    d. It forecasts future events that could cause stress.

3. **Which of the following best describes coping mechanisms based on moon signs?**

    a. They are universal techniques applicable to all signs.

    b. They are specific strategies tailored according to each moon sign's characteristics.

    c. They are outdated methods with no scientific basis.

    d. They only work during a full moon.

4. **What extra stress relief techniques can be derived from sun signs?**

    a. They help decide the most stressful days of the week.

b. They provide insights into personality traits, which can guide self-care practices.

c. They forecast potential health issues.

d. They suggest suitable exercise routines.

5. **How does the 6th House in a birth chart contribute to daily rituals for self-care?**

    a. It suggests appropriate times for meditation and relaxation.

    b. It provides insight into dietary needs and physical health routines.

    c. It shows potential challenges in relationships.

    d. It reveals hidden talents or skills.

## *Answers*

1. b. It shows our core unconscious stressors.
2. b. It aids in understanding your emotional nature and reactions.
3. b. They are specific strategies tailored according to each moon sign's characteristics.
4. b. They provide insights into personality traits, which can guide self-care practices.
5. b. It provides insight into dietary needs and physical health routines.

Chapter 8:

# Attracting Love and Happiness

Questions about love and relationships possibly lie first or second in the minds of those seeking guidance. I know I've used astrology to that end, and so have those who have consulted me.

Whether we are single or in a relationship, we're naturally curious about the direction it's likely to take.

## Venus, Love, and Relationships

Love can be expressed in countless ways, from bold announcements on social media to quiet, thoughtful acts such as preparing a favorite meal or helping around the house. Some people express affection in deeply emotional, sentimental ways, while for others, love is about maintaining a strong physical bond, whether through playful public displays or intimacy behind closed doors. All of these expressions are heavily influenced by where Venus, the planet of love, sits in your birth chart.

Venus shapes how you give and receive love, making each person's approach to affection unique.

Once you identify the zodiac sign that governs your Venus, you can enhance the qualities associated with it. By consciously connecting with your Venus sign, you nurture its energy, and strengthen your romantic intentions. Knowing what your emotional needs are and being able to fulfill them yourself opens the door to attracting the right type of person for you to appreciate and love.

- **Earth Venus**: Those with Venus in an earth sign are sensual and deliberate in love, often taking their time to commit and are selective in their romantic choices. They appreciate the physical and practical aspects of relationships, enjoying both touch and tangible expressions of love, like gifts. If an earth Venus has been hinting at something they've had their eye on, such as a simple yet meaningful object like a houseplant, getting it for them is a way to show love and appreciation.

- **Water Venus**: A water Venus brings deep emotional connection to their relationships. They are intuitive and attuned to their partner's feelings, often without needing words. They're devoted and loyal, offering a steady emotional support that can last a lifetime. For them, love is a profound, unspoken bond.

- **Fire Venus**: When Venus is in a fire sign, expect passion, excitement, and a competitive edge. They thrive on the thrill of the chase and can be impulsive in matters of the heart and won't hesitate to declare their love early on. They crave spontaneity, surprises, and unpredictability to keep the flames alive.

- **Air Venus**: Those with an air Venus bring a breezy, adaptable energy to love. They are more focused on intellectual stimulation and freedom within a relationship. It's up to you to capture their attention through fun and unconventional experiences. They prefer to keep things light and refreshing, finding balance in their connections.

- **Retrograde Venus**: When Venus goes retrograde, it can prompt a period of reflection on relationships, encouraging us to reassess our desires and how we can improve our romantic lives. For each Venus sign, this period serves as a reminder to reconnect with the love language that resonates most deeply.

## Mars and Relationships

Mars is the primal force driving our romantic pursuits, urging us to express our desires and take bold actions. As Mars moves through each of the zodiac signs, it brings its own intensity, shaping how we assert ourselves and experience passion in our relationships. This planet plays a crucial role in influencing attraction, stirring up intimate desires, and motivating us to chase after what we want.

Ever felt a spark when meeting someone new? That's Mars at work; its fiery energy lights the path toward romantic interests. In relationships, Mars acts as a magnetic force, pulling us into the thrilling excitement of early romance. When Mars is strong in your birth chart, it signals a confident, passionate nature, ready to pursue love with intense and vibrant energy.

A dominant Mars can also come with challenges such as impatience, impulsiveness, and aggression. When two people have compatible Mars signs, they share a natural rhythm of passion and desire aligning effortlessly, and creating a relationship full of mutual support and fiery enthusiasm. Together, they motivate each other, fanning the flames of excitement and harmony.

Mars expresses itself differently depending on the type of sign.

- Fire signs identify what they want and unreservedly pursue it.
- Water signs may feel shy or struggle to openly express their feelings.
- Air signs are quick-witted and energized by communication and the exchange of ideas.
- Earth signs prefer a steady, long-term approach to love but may find it difficult to demonstrate affection openly.
- If Mars is retrograde in your birth chart, it often indicates a suppression of sexual desires or may cause confusion about preferences, especially if other astrological challenges are present.

When Mars itself goes retrograde, it can bring frustrations in our relationships. It also gives us a chance to slow down, reassess our desires, and patiently work through issues with perseverance, ultimately strengthening our relationship.

## *The Interplay Between Venus and Mars*

Understanding the interplay between Mars and Venus offers valuable insights into the forces that shape love, desire, and attraction in our relationships.

Mars embodies passion, drive, and action, while Venus symbolizes love, beauty, and harmony.

### *Mars: The Fire of Passion*

Mars, the planet of action and desire, is central to how we express individuality, pursue romance, and assert our sexual drive in relationships.

- **Taking Initiative and Assertiveness**: Mars governs how we take charge in love. Its placement in a birth chart reveals how assertive we are in pursuing our desires and taking the lead in relationships. People with strong Mars energy are usually bold, direct, and proactive when it comes to romantic love.

- **Sexual Drive and Compatibility**: Where Mars sits in a birth chart can point to our preferred sexual style, levels of passion, and how we connect physically. Understanding the Mars energy in both partners helps create a harmonious and fulfilling intimate connection.

- **Handling Conflict and Power Struggles**: When Mars energy becomes excessive, assertiveness can turn into aggression or an overpowering need to dominate. Learning to channel this energy in constructive ways helps in resolving conflicts while maintaining a balanced relationship.

### *Venus: The Essence of Love*

Venus, as the planet of love and beauty, significantly impacts how we experience affection, partnership, and emotional fulfillment.

- **Attraction and Romantic Chemistry**: Its placement highlights the qualities we are drawn to in love. By understanding your Venus sign and your partner's, you can unlock the chemistry that fuels romantic attraction.

- **Building Emotional Connection and Intimacy**: Venus reveals how we express affection and connect deeply with others. Its energy fosters nurturing, harmony, and the desire for a meaningful, lasting bond with a partner.

- **Values and Relationship Harmony**: Venus shapes how we seek balance within partnerships. Understanding each partner's Venus energy allows you to align your values and create a mutually supportive, fulfilling dynamic.

- **Love Communication and Expression**: Venus influences the way we express love and affection, how we communicate in relationships, and our desire for peaceful, harmonious interactions. Recognizing how you and your partner's Venus energies communicate can enhance your connection and foster a more loving atmosphere.

### *Finding Balance Between Mars and Venus*

A harmonious relationship thrives when Mars and Venus energies are in balance which is essential for a fulfilling connection.

- Open Communication: Discuss desires, needs, and expectations openly to ensure both partners feel heard and valued.

- Embrace Both Planet's Qualities: Recognize and appreciate the assertive qualities of Mars alongside the nurturing energy of Venus.

- Respect and Appreciation: Allow space for each partner to verbalize their wants and needs while respecting their boundaries and feelings.

- Active Listening: Cultivate empathy and active listening to resolve conflicts peacefully and foster mutual understanding.

Balancing these powerful energies can lead to a relationship that is not only passionate but also deeply connected, harmonious, and lasting.

# Synastry Charts

When the charts of two people are combined in a relationship reading, we can determine similarities, difficulties, and issues that they couple may experience. This is based on the comparison of the two charts, which show us where planets, signs, and houses are aligned and where there are weak facets.

When charts aren't compatible, it means that you may have a tougher time navigating your relationship than expected. But remember, astrology also gives you the information you need to make it work.

## *How to Compare Charts*

In synastry, your zodiac sign reflects your core essence, and how it aligns with someone else's can shape the dynamics of your connection. Drawing up a page (like an excel spreadsheet) that contains the necessary details will make it easier to compare and understand these. Your page will consist of five columns across and 12 lines down.

- First column: List the houses from 1st to 12th.
- Second column: Note the planet and sign that was in each house as per your birth chart; include the degree the planet was in.
- Third column: Record your partner's planet and sign that was in each house as per their birth chart, including the degree the planet was in.
- Fourth column: Mark where there are similarities in terms of planets between the two charts and compare degrees.
- Fifth column: Make a note of where the elements appear in each chart.

When planets in both charts fall within five degrees of each other, creating a tight to moderate orb, they are said to align closely, suggesting a harmonious and powerful connection.

## *Compatibility Based on Planetary Placements*

When celestial bodies from both charts align in synastry, they provide clues about how the relationship unfolds.

- Mercury: Communication is crucial, and open dialogue helps the relationship grow.
- Venus: Romance, pleasure, and good times are abundant, creating a joyful connection.
- Mars: Intense energy and passion are directed toward each other.
- Jupiter: Growth, exploration, and shared intellectual pursuits bring excitement.
- Saturn: Challenges and lessons arise, but Saturn helps create a stable, long-lasting bond.
- Uranus: Stability may be lacking, but the connection is full of surprises and spontaneity.
- Neptune: Dreams and ideas are shared, with unconditional support for each other.
- Pluto: Deep transformation is possible, though power struggles may need to be addressed.
- Sun: Enhances the qualities of the planets it touches in another's chart.
- Moon: Creates a lasting emotional bond, providing comfort and security in the relationship.

- North Node: This connection speaks to how you'll shape each other's future, indicating growth and purpose together.
- South Node: A past-life connection is implied, showing how your relationship draws on karmic patterns and lessons.

## *The Role of Houses in Synastry*

When your key planets, such as the sun, moon, or rising sign, fall into a significant house in the other person's chart, it indicates a meaningful bond. Other planets also play a role in telling the story of the relationship.

- First House: You feel deeply seen and recognized by each other, fostering a strong connection.
- Second House: Financial dynamics may play a role, and they may boost your sense of self-worth.
- Third House: Communication flows naturally, with ease and understanding.
- Fourth House: This person might remind you of home, creating a sense of comfort and familiarity.
- Fifth House: Fun and creativity thrive as you inspire each other to enjoy life.
- Sixth House: Mutual support is key, and you could even bond through routines like exercise.
- Seventh House: This could signal partnership, whether in romance or rivalry.
- Eighth House: There's a magnetic attraction, with deep growth and transformation in the mix.

- Ninth House: Shared interests in travel, philosophy, and learning foster connection.
- Tenth House: Your roles in each other's careers may be significant, offering support or competing ambitions.
- Eleventh House: Friendship, shared causes, and humanitarian pursuits are central.
- Twelfth House: Secrets and hidden dynamics may emerge, especially in clandestine relationships.

There is another chart that can be used for relationships that goes beyond just compatibility.

## Composite Charts

One of the most insightful charts in relationship astrology is the composite chart, which blends two people's energies into one unified blueprint.

Imagine what it would look like if two people merged in perfect harmony or struck a great balance between their strengths and weaknesses. A composite chart serves as a cosmic guide, revealing how two energies come together as one.

- Composite charts focus on the partnership as a single unit. Instead of comparing two separate charts, it creates a new one, resembling a birth chart but with one set of planetary positions and aspects that symbolize the relationship's unique dynamics.
- A synastry chart determines your level of compatibility with another person by doing a side-by-side comparison of two birth charts and examining the aspects and angles formed between the planets and houses in each chart.

A composite chart is a single chart on its own, representing the shared energy of the relationship and determines how it's likely to progress.

## *Compiling Composite Charts*

This special chart is created by calculating the midpoint between each corresponding planet in the two birth charts, generating a third chart; a perfect blend of both individuals' energies. It's like overlaying two charts and finding the middle ground then creating an entirely new map of the relationship illustrating the spiritual potential and challenges of uniting with another person.

Picture two suns from different charts being overlaid, then placing a new sun right in the middle; this is essentially how a composite chart is formed. More precisely, it's calculated by determining the midpoint between each person's planetary positions, resulting in a new chart that represents the relationship as a whole.

## *Composite Chart Revelations*

Like a celestial roadmap, the composite chart reveals the unique needs of a partnership, offering guidance on how to keep it thriving. Like any other chart, the energies present in a composite chart can be worked with; the difficult facets offer opportunities for growth, while the positive ones can be enhanced and nurtured.

Because relationships evolve over time, certain aspects and placements in the composite chart may not be immediately apparent when the relationship begins. More advanced techniques, such as examining transits to the composite chart or progressing it beyond the initial meeting, can offer deeper insights into how the relationship unfolds. However, the composite chart itself can provide key indicators of how two people begin projects together, navigate changes, and even how the relationship may conclude. It reveals both the visible and hidden characteristics of a relationship.

To explain a little further: The 12th House in the composite chart often symbolizes endings, and the composite sun becomes more prominent as the relationship moves into deeper stages of commitment. The 7th and 8th Houses also come into sharper focus as a relationship grows in intimacy and mutual responsibility.

### *Aspects*

When analyzing a composite chart, it's important to consider aspects; namely, whether they're predominant, scarce, or unaspected. An unaspected sun might suggest that the relationship feels directionless and uncertain. Meanwhile, planets in aspect to the composite ascendant highlight the active, visible energies the couple experiences in their daily life together. These reveal their automatic reactions, natural defenses, how they handle routine challenges, and are the energies most noticeable to those around them.

When planets form harmonious aspects to the composite ascendant, they can indicate a couple's ease in managing issues related to that particular planet. These energies are often well-received by others, creating a sense of natural compatibility. This can, however, put pressure on the couple to live up to the perceived image.

## The Role of the 7th House in Relationships

Relationships possess the ability to transform our lives in profound ways. Lifelong connections, intense brief twin flame encounters, or business alliances that start with a simple handshake can shift our paths. These bonds provide lessons, purpose, and direct us toward our highest spiritual potential.

The 7th House governs the realm of relationships. While the playful 5th House deals with casual affairs and fleeting attractions, and the 8th House relates to sexuality and intimacy, the 7th House is where we explore deeper, more committed connections. It represents the partnerships we invest in; romantic, professional, or otherwise. The 7th House reveals how we form emotional security through lasting connections.

### *Partnerships*

The 7th House is primarily associated with partnerships and romance, but it covers other important relationships. It sheds light on who we choose to team up with. When analyzing the planets in the 7th House, it offers insights into your potential partner's characteristics and your overall approach to relationships.

### *Contracts*

This house also governs contracts and agreements, including marriage, divorce, business dealings, and ownership rights. It may touch on adversarial relationships or how we are perceived publicly. With challenging planetary aspects in this house, caution is needed before entering into legal or binding agreements.

### *Self and Others*

Relationships often act as mirrors, reflecting both our best qualities and our deepest flaws. The 7th House helps us see these reflections, encouraging self-awareness and growth. It teaches us to balance our strengths and shadows, providing insight into how we relate to others and how those relationships serve our personal development.

Astrology, much like relationships, is layered and complex. Finding a soulmate involves more than just looking at your 7th House. The 7th House, however, can highlight what one truly needs for a balanced, harmonious relationship.

Positive aspects such as trines, conjunctions, or sextiles can indicate long-lasting emotional fulfillment and shared goals. When both partners have favorable connections to each other's 7th House, it strengthens the potential for a harmonious, enduring relationship.

By complementing each other's strengths and compensating for weaknesses, these aspects help build a solid foundation for mutual growth and fulfillment.

# Attracting Love and Joy

We cannot attract the right type of love if do not practice self-love. Loving ourselves is different from being vain, self-centered, or selfish. It is accepting who we are and loving ourselves unconditionally. Like many other people, there are things we sometimes wish we could change. It may be physical matters such as our hair, nose, or body type, but could also include personality traits like over-thinking, being critical, or a quick temper.

Once we are comfortable in our own skin, we can do a few things to attract the partner that complements us best. I've heard time and again that when asked what we want in a partner, we often speak about what we don't want. When we focus on what we don't want, that's what we attract.

Make a list of your ideal partner's characteristics, the way you want to be treated, and the dynamics of the relationship. Are you looking for someone to nurture you or to explore with? Maybe it's a balance of both. Is it passion and excitement or someone to cuddle and watch movies with that you seek?

Would you have common interests or pursue individual pleasures, giving each other space? Also consider whether your ideal match is a good listener, shows respect, is trustworthy, and all the other boxes you want ticked.

## *Visualizations*

This is a great way to attract a partner. Play a scene through your mind while drifting off to sleep or meditating using the attributes you've listed as desirable. Keep playing pleasant scenarios whenever you find yourself thinking about it. A word of caution: Don't put someone you know or a face to your visualizations. We all have free will, and you don't want to affect someone else's. You may well attract that person, but they are seldom the right fit.

### *Affirmations*

These are one of my favorite ways of attracting what I'm looking for. Make sure you word them positively and don't use negative words. For example, saying, "I want a partner who doesn't cheat," includes the words "want" and "doesn't" which have negative associations. Instead, rephrase it: "I have room in my life for a faithful partner."

### *Chakras*

Everywhere you look, you may be referred to the heart chakra, and yes, I agree, balancing and opening your heart chakra may attract love, but if your other chakras are blown or blocked, it's going to have a knock-on effect. Make sure all seven are in harmony. This can be done through meditations, crystals, color therapy, and mantras to mention a few.

### *Crystals*

They can be used to balance your chakras, to attract opportunities, and for protection. Five crystals commonly associated with the heart chakra are listed below.

- Rhodonite: Helps heal emotional trauma and prepares you to open yourself to new love. Wear it or keep it next to your bed.
- Garnet: Can attract new love when carried around, or to add spice to a relationship, keep it in the bedroom.
- Moonstone: Promotes calm and helps verbalize emotions. It also opens you up to consciously connecting at a higher level.
- Sodalite: Connected to the throat chakra, it can help with communication and expressing your feelings, leading to trust and deeper connections.

- Rose Quartz: Always associated with unconditional love in all forms, this crystal is worn by many to attract love and to maintain harmony.

Of course, we may have love and relationship lessons to learn, which could see us still attracting, or not attracting, people not meant to be in our future. If that seems to be the case, then perhaps you can turn your attention to other areas of your life.

## Progression Quiz

1. **Which planet is known to influence love and relationships in astrology?**

    a. Mars

    b. Venus

    c. Jupiter

    d. Saturn

2. **What is the role of Mars in relationships according to astrology?**

    a. It represents love and harmony.

    b. It signifies communication skills.

    c. It symbolizes action, desire, and competitive drive.

    d. It stands for luck and fortune.

3. **What is a synastry chart used for in astrology?**

    a. To predict future events.

    b. To compare two people's charts for compatibility.

c. To determine your career path.

d. To find lost objects.

4. **What does the 7th House represent in astrological terms?**

   a. Career and public reputation.

   b. Home life and family.

   c. Love, marriage, and partnerships.

   d. Personal development and self-improvement.

5. **How can zodiac signs be used to enhance relationships, according to this chapter?**

   a. By predicting future events.

   b. By understanding personality traits and improving communication.

   c. By determining financial success.

   d. By choosing the right career path.

## *Answers*

1. b. Venus

2. c. It symbolizes action, desire, and competitive drive.

3. b. To compare two people's charts for compatibility.

4. c. Love, marriage, and partnerships.

5. b. By understanding personality traits and improving communication.

Chapter 9:

# Manifesting Success, Wealth, and Abundance

We've all heard that timing is the key to success. Whether we're navigating the stock exchange, getting married, changing careers, or moving house, we usually take the time to think and plan beforehand. One of the most important aspects we consider is whether the timing is right.

Astrology can offer some insight when planning big changes. Earlier, the use of planetary positions, lunar phases, and planetary hours in our day-to-day decisions were covered. But wait! There's more!

## Manifesting Success

When manifesting success, it is important that we understand what we want as well as our strengths and weaknesses, our interests and passions, and we are ready to put in the effort. Sitting on the couch watching reruns on TV won't have our dream jobs falling in our laps. Applying for a lifesaving job when we fear water and can't swim is only going to increase the fear. If that is what we want to do, perhaps swimming lessons, a lifeguard course, and seeing a therapist first may prepare us.

### *The 10th House and Success*

The 10th House in astrology is deeply connected to career, ambitions, and public standing. This house represents our professional life, the path to success, and the way we are viewed by society. It's a crucial part of the astrological chart, highlighting our social status, public roles, and achievements. In career astrology, the 10th House reveals the trajectory we might follow in our work life, how we will be recognized, and which strengths will help us reach our professional goals.

- Career Path: The 10th House outlines our successes in the working world. It maps out our aspirations and rise within our chosen field.

- Public Image: This house reflects how we are perceived by others, influencing both reputation and social standing. It speaks to status and prestige, showing what contributes to our image in society.

- Leadership: The 10th House deals with management positions, decision-making, and the responsibilities we assume in the professional environment.

- Long-Term Goals: Representing long-term ambitions, this house signifies the efforts made to achieve career milestones and professional advancement.

- Contribution to Society: The 10th House shows our role and influence in society, highlighting our impact on others and our contributions through public service, social responsibility, or professional interaction.

The 10th House is linked to Capricorn and the planet Saturn, both of which emphasize discipline, responsibility, and a methodical approach to career. Capricorn encourages a practical and structured path, while Saturn's influence promotes perseverance, patience, and determination in pursuing professional success.

### *Maximizing the Potential of Your 10th House*

To harness the full potential of the 10th House, we must approach our career with intention and focus. This involves setting clear, long-term goals, investing in professional development, and continuously learning. Networking, effective self-expression, and managing our public image are also essential. Leadership and management skills will help unlock the rewards of the 10th House, creating a firm foundation for success and recognition in our career journey. Taking these steps can lead to a more rewarding and fulfilling professional life, fully utilizing the opportunities presented by the 10th House.

## Consult Saturn and Jupiter

Both Saturn and Jupiter have a role to play when it comes to success and prosperity. It may seem that these two planets are at odds; however, they counter each other perfectly, offering balance in these areas.

### *Saturn's Broad Influence*

Saturn's influence in a natal chart symbolizes where we encounter obstacles but also where we can experience profound growth through perseverance. Known as the planet of time and karma, Saturn nudges us toward maturity and responsibility. While its energy may manifest as challenges or restrictions, it ultimately provides a foundation for lasting success through disciplined effort and dedication.

### *Boundaries, Resilience, and Persistence*

Often viewed as a stern teacher, Saturn forces us to confront boundaries in key areas such as career, relationships, and personal development. However, rather than seeing its presence as a burden, it can be embraced as an opportunity for resilience and growth. Saturn's lessons, though demanding, help build stability and inner strength. Its placement in the chart reveals where persistence, thoughtful planning, and strategic effort can yield great rewards.

### *Discipline and Intellect*

Astrologically, Saturn governs Capricorn and Aquarius, instilling discipline and structure in Capricorn while fostering intellectual depth and innovation in Aquarius. Saturn's transits, particularly significant ones like the Saturn return, mark pivotal moments of life reassessment, requiring deep reflection and realignment. It also heavily influences career matters, encouraging systematic approaches, as well as relationships, which demand maturity and long-term commitment.

### *Favorable Positions*

When Saturn forms positive aspects, such as trines or sextiles, it enhances resilience and careful planning, offering a clear path to accomplishment. Strong house placements, especially in the 3rd, 6th, 10th, and 11th Houses, further reinforce progress in areas like career, social connections, and personal development. In Libra, where Saturn is exalted, it encourages a balanced approach to decision-making, promoting leaders who value fairness and responsibility.

Saturn's transits and progressions often mark critical phases of growth, though they require patience and sustained effort. Its aspects, whether supportive or challenging, shape personal evolution, contributing to a life marked by discipline, endurance, and ultimately, success.

## *Jupiter's Broad Influence in Life*

Jupiter's influence extends across a range of life areas, from personal growth and wisdom to wealth and fortune. Jupiter's impact is considered deeply beneficial. It rules over Sagittarius and Pisces, reaches its peak strength in Cancer, and finds itself at a disadvantage in Capricorn.

### *Wisdom, Knowledge, and Intellectual Growth*

A strong Jupiter in a natal chart is a marker of intellect, wisdom, and a deep interest in learning. Those under its positive influence are naturally drawn to education, exploring new philosophies, and broadening their understanding of the world. These people often possess a curious and inquisitive mind, eager to delve into different subjects and cultures.

### *Growth, Expansion, and Prosperity*

Jupiter's connection with expansion and abundance brings opportunities for growth in both personal and professional spheres. It encourages us to seize opportunities, pursue our ambitions with optimism, and use our abilities and resources to achieve success. Jupiter's influence fosters confidence, urging us to step into new experiences that lead to prosperity and fulfillment.

Jupiter also highlights the importance of wise mentors and teachers in life. Those under its guidance often find themselves connected to knowledgeable individuals who provide valuable insight, helping them navigate life's complexities and encouraging their growth.

### *Ethical Values and Moral Integrity*

Jupiter governs the moral compass, urging us to uphold principles of fairness, honesty, and righteousness in all aspects of life. Those strongly influenced by Jupiter are known for their ethical conduct and transparency, striving to make decisions that reflect high moral standards in both personal and professional relationships. A commitment to integrity is central to Jupiter's energy, encouraging people to lead a life rooted in justice and righteousness.

## *Maximizing Jupiter's Positive Influence*

To fully harness Jupiter's auspicious energy for growth, prosperity, and wisdom, consider the following approaches:

- **Cultivate a Love for Learning and Wisdom**: Embrace a mindset of continuous learning. Explore new philosophies, spiritual teachings, and diverse cultural perspectives. Engaging with intellectual pursuits and expanding your knowledge will not only stimulate your mind but also deepen your understanding of the world and your place within it.

- **Embrace Growth and Prosperity Opportunities**: Stay open to opportunities that promote personal and professional growth. Align your goals with your talents and passions, and use your skills and resources to build success. Jupiter's energy encourages optimism and confidence, so pursuing your aspirations with enthusiasm will lead to greater fulfillment and abundance.

- **Uphold Integrity and Moral Principles**: Commit to living a life of integrity, honesty, and ethical behavior. In your decisions and relationships, make choices that reflect your core values and principles. Acting with fairness and righteousness will allow you to navigate life's challenges with a clear conscience and remain aligned with Jupiter's benevolent energy.

# The Part of Fortune and Divine Luck

The Part of Fortune, often referred to as the *Lot of Fortune* or *Pars Fortuna*, is a unique element in your natal chart that is calculated by factoring in your sun, moon, and ascendant signs, commonly known as the *big three*. Unlike celestial bodies that are visible in the sky, the Part of Fortune is an abstract point, rooted in an ancient system called the *Arabic Parts*. This method involves measuring the distance between two planets and adding it to the position of the third, typically the ascendant, to generate a *lot*. This point is believed to reflect your potential for success, hinting at how destiny, fate, and chance will influence your life.

## *What Does the Part of Fortune Represent?*

The Part of Fortune is associated with progress, wealth, and overall abundance. Everyone has their own Part of Fortune, though some may find it easier to align with their cosmic purpose than others. The placement of this point in your natal chart—both in terms of its zodiac sign and house—can reveal areas where you're likely to excel, find happiness, and achieve personal mastery. As the Part of Fortune is closely connected to your soul's evolutionary journey, it can be particularly sensitive to change, especially when activated by key transits or other celestial events. During these moments, it may open doors for you to harness your potential.

### *How to Discover Your Part of Fortune*

The Part of Fortune appears in your chart as a wheel with an *X* in the center. It's a calculated point, determined by a formula based on whether you were born during the day or night. If you were born during daylight, meaning the sun is in Houses 7 through 12, your Part of Fortune is calculated as: Rising sign - sun sign + moon sign. Conversely, if you were born at night, with the sun in Houses 1 through 6, the equation shifts to: Rising sign - moon sign + sun sign.

### *The Part of Fortune in the 12 Zodiac Signs*

Once you've identified the zodiac sign that your Part of Fortune occupies, you can begin to explore potential career paths and personal growth strategies that align with your goals.

- Aries: Taking risks and pursuing independence, whether through entrepreneurship or leadership roles, will lead to fulfillment. Careers in physical activities or adrenaline-driven fields, like firefighting or stunt performing, are ideal.
- Taurus: You thrive in fields where your loyalty shines, such as art, music, or culinary arts. Financial stability is crucial, making banking or investing viable paths for success.
- Gemini: Careers involving writing, speaking, or presenting, whether as a content creator, news anchor, or performer, are where you'll excel.
- Cancer: Work that aligns with family values, caregiving, or creating a comforting environment, such as teaching, social work, or real estate, is best suited for you.
- Leo: Whether you're a performer or leader, you need to be in a role where your confidence and charisma can shine.
- Virgo: Careers in wellness, writing, research, or even data analysis will allow you to showcase your strengths.
- Libra: Working in fields that require relationship-building, such as law, fashion, or interior design, will help you thrive.
- Scorpio: Careers involving transformation, psychology, or detective work suit your mysterious and powerful nature.
- Sagittarius: Careers that offer variety, such as education, travel, or spiritual guidance, will help you feel fulfilled.

- Capricorn: Climbing the corporate ladder or working in finance, business, or science will allow you to demonstrate your expertise.

- Aquarius: Jobs that involve technology, social reform, or humanitarian efforts, where you can break away from tradition, are ideal for you.

- Pisces: Whether through the arts, counseling, or healing professions, your fluid and intuitive nature leads you to success when you trust your instincts.

## The 2nd House and Money

The 2nd House in astrology represents our connection to money, values, possessions, and self-worth, shaping how we interact with material resources and our sense of personal value. This house offers insight into our financial habits and what we consider truly valuable in life.

It's the place to look when trying to understand what boosts someone's confidence, what they value, and what builds their self-esteem.

Known as the *house of practical magic*, the 2nd House influences our relationship with comfort and pleasure. It's also the first of the three Earth houses, which govern our material security, alongside the 6th and 10th Houses.

This is where the foundation for earned income and financial management is established. It shares similar qualities with Taurus, the zodiac's second sign, making this house one where personal beliefs and traditions are often firmly upheld. Also referred to as the *house of possessions*, it reveals how we handle wealth, our attitude toward saving and spending, and what we hold dear.

### *The 2nd House and Practical Knowledge*

This house extends beyond thought into practical knowledge, reflecting our skills in budgeting, saving, spending, and investment. It's about turning dreams of wealth into tangible realities. The 2nd House shows how we can leverage our talents and passions in practical ways that benefit our financial life. It represents the drive to create a life of value and meaning, taking us from wanting something to actually having it.

### *Challenges and Lessons in the 2nd House*

Material wealth often comes with its own set of challenges and lessons. The desire to be financially secure is natural, but it's easy to become overly attached to material possessions or to tie self-worth to what we own. This can lead to a distorted view of both ourselves and others, placing too much importance on wealth and status.

That's why balance is crucial in the 2nd House. Staying grounded and cultivating gratitude and generosity ensures that wealth doesn't dominate your identity or interactions.

### *The 2nd House and Personal Legacy*

The 2nd House also plays a significant role in shaping our legacy, hinting at what we'll leave behind, whether material assets, inheritance, or the values regarding money and abundance. This house encourages us to think about how our financial approach affects others and what kind of influence we have on the way people in our circle perceive wealth.

In our modern capitalist society, the 2nd House prompts us to reflect on our relationship with money, value, and materialism, making it more relevant than ever.

## Using Jupiter to Attract Abundance

The connection between Jupiter and Thursday is rooted in ancient planetary associations, with Thursday deriving its name from *Thor's day*, linked to the Norse god of thunder, Thor. Much like Jupiter, Thor symbolizes power, storms, and protection. The influence of Jupiter over Thursday imbues the day with energies of abundance, growth, and expansive thinking. Thursday becomes a time for embracing Jupiter's cosmic forces, making it an ideal day to focus on opportunities, think big, and foster a mindset of prosperity and success.

### *Techniques to Harness Jupiter's Power*

#### *Manifestation Practices*

- Wealth Affirmations: Begin your day with affirmations like, "I am open to receiving wealth," setting a positive tone for financial growth.
- Vision Board: Create a board with images and quotes representing your financial goals, keeping it visible to focus on manifesting success.
- Abundance Journaling: Write as if you've already achieved your financial dreams, describing emotions and opportunities to align with your goals.

#### *Visualization Techniques*

- Future Wealth: Visualize living a life of financial abundance, engaging all your senses to make it vivid.
- Money Magnet: Meditate and imagine a magnetic field drawing in wealth and opportunities.

- Jupiter's Guidance: Envision Jupiter guiding your financial journey, showering your ventures with golden light and positive energy.

***Enhancing Thursday With Colors, Scents, and Gems***

- Colors (Purple and Green): Wear these colors or add them to your surroundings to align with Jupiter's energy.
- Scents (Juniper and Pine): Use candles, diffusers, or scented products to enhance prosperity and vitality.
- Gems (Amethyst and Green Aventurine): Wear or meditate with these stones to attract financial success and spiritual growth.

It must be stressed that no one element of astrology is going to bring good fortune, predict your future, or tell you about yourself. It is a combination of variables that make you who you are and had influence over your life. However, making use of astrological tools may provide you with an advantage.

## Progression Quiz

1. **What is the astrological house that is often associated with career success?**

    a. The 5th House

    b. The 10th House

    c. The 2nd House

    d. The 8th House

2. **Which two planets' positions are considered crucial in balancing discipline and opportunity for manifesting success?**

    a. Mars and Venus

    b. Jupiter and Saturn

    c. Mercury and Neptune

    d. Uranus and Pluto

3. **What is the Part of Fortune often referred to in astrology?**

    a. A specific alignment of all planets.

    b. A point in the horoscope that relates to divine luck.

    c. An asteroid belt influencing your fortune.

    d. A particular phase of the moon.

4. **Which astrological house signifies your relationship with money?**

    a. The 7th House

    b. The 12th House

    c. The 1st House

    d. The 2nd House

5. **How can you use Jupiter's influence to attract abundance, according to astrology principles?**

    a. By focusing on its position during full moon nights only.

    b. By aligning it with other planet's positions.

    c. By understanding its transit through different houses.

d. By wearing gemstones related to Jupiter.

## *Answers*

1. b. The 10th House
2. b. Jupiter and Saturn
3. b. A point in the horoscope that relates to divine luck.
4. d. The 2nd House
5. c. By understanding its transit through different houses.

Chapter 10:

# An Action Plan

There are yet more celestial movements to take into consideration when planning ahead. Doing so can help you prepare for the coming days, weeks, months, and year ahead. We explore some of the less familiar facets in this chapter.

## Draconic Chart

The Draconic zodiac, differs from traditional and modern astrology in that, instead of basing a chart on sun signs, charts are based on the lunar nodes and explore the realms of emotion, memory, and the subconscious. Its name, derived from Latin, refers to the lunar North and South Nodes. These nodes signify the points where the solar and lunar paths intersect, intertwining the conscious energy of the sun with the emotional depth of the moon.

The nodes consist of the True Node, which considers the moon's orbital fluctuations, and the Mean Node, which provides an average of its position. The True Node occasionally stations and moves direct for a few days each month, while the Mean Node remains perpetually retrograde. Their positions are usually very close to one another.

The Draconic zodiac also comprises of 12 signs, each spanning 30 degrees. The traditional zodiac commences at 0° Aries (the Vernal Point) and highlights psychological characteristics, whereas the Draconic zodiac begins at the North Node (0° Aries) and focuses on unconscious influences and memories. The interplay between these zodiacs is evident in the planetary connections, where Draconic planets influence the traditional chart, unveiling hidden aspects of one's personality.

The nodes traverse retrograde through the zodiac over approximately 18.5 years, spending about 1.5 years in each sign. Transits through the Draconic zodiac can be transformative, often bringing past issues to light and offering closure to unresolved matters.

The North Node signifies the qualities we aim to cultivate, while the South Node reveals our ingrained tendencies. The South Node isn't inherently negative; it can represent habitual behaviors that we must transcend to embrace the attributes of the North Node. This axis is frequently referred to as the *path of the soul.*

## *The Role of Vertex*

While most celestial placements reveal insights into your innate personality, one specific element illuminates how you are perceived by others: The astrological vertex. Unlike other astrological concepts that revolve around planets or stars, the vertex is determined by the intersection of two imaginary circles in the heavens: The ecliptic. The ecliptic symbolizes the sun's journey from our perspective on Earth and intersects with the prime vertical, which splits the celestial sphere into its front and back halves. This intersection is where the astrological vertex is positioned, often appearing on the right side of your chart. It's typically located anywhere from the 5th to the 8th Houses, and is recognizable in your chart by a *Vx* symbol.

The positioning of this vertex indicates the way we interact and connect with others, aligning with the characteristics of the right hemisphere of your birth chart. The left side of our birth chart reveals our inner self and the houses related to personal matters, while the right side focuses on public life and interpersonal dynamics.

Your ascendant appears on the left side, representing the outward persona you present to the world. Directly across from this point is the descendant, which signifies your relationships with others. Essentially, the astrological vertex can be viewed as a secondary descendant, reflecting external forces influencing your life. Events linked to the vertex are seen as occurring beyond your control or intent, emphasizing its connection to destiny and unexpected life experiences.

Unlike the traditional descendant, which relates to the activities, environments, and individuals you are drawn to, the vertex concerns external factors that you may inadvertently attract. A vertex can remain dormant in your chart until it is triggered by a celestial event, a person, place, or other event, at which time it will be activated.

The time of the placement of a vertex in a particular sign will reflect the characteristics of that sign.

## *The Void of Course Moon*

An intriguing event that is often overlooked, the Void of Course Moon deserves a brief explanation. While it happens more frequently than events like Mercury retrograde, its impact can be equally disruptive.

A Void of Course Moon occurs when the moon, while traveling through a zodiac sign, makes its final significant aspect to other planets before entering the next sign. This period can range from a few minutes to several hours, and astrologers caution against initiating important actions or decisions during this time. The moon is considered to be in a rest phase, where its influence is diminished, leading to outcomes that may differ from expectations. Here's how you might notice its effects:

You may experience feelings of emotional detachment or lack of connection with others. Tasks started during a Void of Course Moon could take longer to finish or may require revisions, and choices made during this time often need to be reconsidered later.

### *Activities to Avoid*

Here are a few things best avoided during a Void of Course Moon:

- Signing contracts: Unexpected outcomes that work against you may occur.
- Important meetings: Communication may not go as smoothly as desired.
- Introducing anything new: They may be rejected or not progress as planned.
- Major purchases: Buyers' remorse could follow.

### *Planetary Influence and Mercury Retrograde vs. Void of Course Moon*

The broader alignment of the planets adds context to the Void of Course Moon's impact. If Mercury is in retrograde at the same time, the disruptions may feel even more pronounced. While both can cause complications, their effects differ.

Mercury retrograde usually disrupts external matters like communication and technology, whereas a Void of Course Moon leads to internal struggles, creating a sense of stagnation.

- Keep it Simple: Focus on routine tasks that don't require significant decisions.
- Self-Reflection: Use this period for introspection, meditation, or catching up on rest.
- Double-Check: If you must schedule something important, triple-check all details to avoid confusion.

## Solar Return Charts

A solar return chart is just as personal as your natal chart. As Earth completes its yearly orbit around the sun, a solar return occurs when the sun reaches the precise degrees and minutes it occupied at the time of your birth. In your natal chart, each planet and luminary is positioned in specific signs and degrees.

When any of these return to that exact spot, it marks a return. In the case of a solar return, this event takes place around your birthday but may differ by a day or two.

A solar return chart is a powerful tool for predicting the energies and events you're likely to encounter in the coming year. Each year, the sun returns to the same zodiac degree but enters a different house with varying aspects to other planets, giving each solar return its own unique dynamic. This shifting cosmic landscape provides insight into the specific themes that will shape your experiences.

The Earth's orbit around the sun doesn't perfectly align with a calendar year, taking roughly 365.25 days to complete its journey. This is why every four years, we observe a leap year, adding an extra day on February 29th to compensate.

The solar return chart reflects these cosmic nuances, offering a personalized forecast for the year ahead.

Key elements to focus on in your solar return chart include:

- **The Sun's Position**: While the sun returns to its natal zodiacal degree, it may occupy a different house. This shift can highlight new areas of focus. For example, if the sun was in the 2nd House (income) at birth but is now in the 7th House (partnerships), it suggests a year centered around relationships.

- **Other Planets**: Take note of how the sun interacts with other planets in the chart. If it's aligned with Venus, expect a love and beauty infused year. An opposition with Mars, however, could signal heightened assertiveness and competition.

- **The Rising Sign**: The sign on the ascendant offers a peek into the year ahead and how you'll face it. If Leo is rising, you may crave luxury and the spotlight. If Aquarius, your focus may shift to technology and group-oriented activities.

- **Ascendant Ruler**: The ruling planet of the ascendant shapes its core energy and plays a key role in defining your approach to the year. Tracking this planet's movements—especially retrograde periods—can give you a deeper understanding of the themes driving your life during the year.

Many astrologers recommend consulting with a professional to help you interpret how your solar return chart interacts with ongoing planetary transits, offering a more detailed forecast for the months ahead.

## Lunar Return Charts

A lunar return occurs when the moon returns to the exact position it held at the time of your birth, creating a chart that reveals insights for the next lunar cycle. Since the moon is the fastest-moving celestial body, we experience a lunar return approximately every 28 days. By tracking your lunar cycles, you can bring suppressed feelings to light and gain clarity into your emotional security.

## *A Short-Term Guide*

Much like a solar return chart forecasts the themes of the upcoming year, the lunar return chart focuses on what will be significant in the coming month. By combining this chart with your birth or solar return charts, you can gain a deeper understanding of how the planets influence your inner and outer worlds. They act as a guide to help you align your focus with the natural ebb and flow of your life.

The best thing about working with lunar return charts is that you can use them to help you plan for the next month. They offer a view into your energy levels, social habits, motivation, and emotional focus for the month ahead.

The moon's placement in your chart can hint at which areas of life will demand the most attention.

- **General**: Other than setting goals, the lunar return chart can guide self-care strategies. It's particularly valuable during times of change, such as moving, job searching, or navigating relationships. It also lets you know whether you're behaving out of emotional reaction and when you might be ready for new opportunities.

- **Spiritual**: Lunar returns serve as a check-in point, revealing which types of spiritual practices or routines might be most beneficial during the upcoming month. They offer guidance on whether you're in a period of receiving spiritual insights or if it's a time to focus on introspective work.

- **Practical Use**: Lunar returns remind us to check in with our emotional state. They can signal whether your energy will be low or if you'll feel the need for solitude. The house in which the moon resides in the return chart can also point to where your emotional priorities lie. For those who practice folk magic or work with the unseen, tuning into lunar cycles can be an essential tool. For someone who is neurodivergent or managing chronic illness, lunar returns provide a structured way to remain connected to both external rhythms and inner feelings.

The day of your lunar return each month acts as a reset button, offering an opportunity to reflect and set new intentions for the next four weeks. It's a powerful time for new mindsets, habits, or priorities to emerge. When you calculate your lunar return chart, you get a snapshot of the planetary alignments and how they impact your emotional landscape.

Take note of the aspects between planets which are crucial, as they reveal what themes may influence you emotionally for the next month.

## Progression Quiz

1. **What is a Draconic chart in astrology?**

    a. A chart that maps the position of the planets at your birth.

    b. A chart that reveals your soul's purpose in this life.

    c. A chart that shows your future predictions based on planetary movements.

    d. A chart that displays the alignment of stars and constellations.

2. **How does the Vertex play a role in astrology?**

    a. It represents our past lives.

    b. It signifies our destiny or fate, often triggered by outside events or people.

    c. It indicates our financial prosperity.

    d. It helps us understand our relationships with pets.

3. **What is meant by "manifesting with planetary hours?"**

   a. Using specific hours associated with different planets for manifesting wants.

   b. Meditating during certain hours when planets are visible.

   c. Sleeping during certain planetary hours to have prophetic dreams.

   d. Eating foods associated with different planets during their ruling hours.

4. **How can the Void of Course Moon be used in astrology?**

   a. To forecast natural disasters.

   b. To avoid starting new projects, making important decisions, or signing contracts, as it's considered an unfavorable time.

   c. To enhance your psychic abilities.

   d. To increase your chances of winning a lottery.

5. **What is a solar return chart used for in astrology?**

   a. To track daily horoscope predictions.

   b. To determine compatibility between two individuals.

   c. To map out key themes and potential challenges or opportunities for each year around your birthday.

   d. To identify suitable gemstones based on one's zodiac sign.

## *Answers*

1. b. A chart that reveals your soul's purpose in this life.
2. b. It signifies our destiny or fate, often triggered by outside events or people.
3. a. Using specific hours associated with different planets for manifesting wants.
4. b. To avoid starting new projects, making important decisions, or signing contracts, as it's considered an unfavorable time.
5. c. To map out key themes and potential challenges or opportunities for each year around your birthday.

Chapter 11:

# Practical Applications

As a new astrologer, you probably have a lot of questions and may find that there are questions you wanted to ask but forgot what they were, or you may have been focused on one area and overlooked another.

You may get distracted midway and lose momentum. As you navigate the beginning of your astrology journey, you can draw up a template to keep on track. You can use it for questions in all areas of life and adapt it to suit you.

# Mrs. Hilda's Recommended Sequence for Your Personal Action Plan and Flowchart Development

Below are recommended questions. Once you begin to interpret charts for others (if that's what you want to do) you can use it to give them a comprehensive chart.

## *General*

- What is my star sign, and does it reflect who I am and indicate my life purpose?
- What is my moon sign, and does it reveal my inner and emotional needs?
- What is my ascendant sign, and how does the world see me?
- What are my elements? Do any dominate? How do they shape me?
- What modalities are in my chart? Are they balanced? How do they affect me?

## *Career and Purpose*

- What sign appears on the cusp of my 10th House (midheaven), and does it reflect my career path and public image?
- What planets appear in my 10th House, and what influence do they have on my professional life?

- Where does Saturn appear, and does it reflect areas of discipline and long-term goals?
- Where does Jupiter appear, and how can I use it for growth and career opportunities?
- What challenging aspects are there to my midheaven or career planets that need my attention?

## *Relationships and Love*

- What sign appears on my cusp, and how will it influence my relationships?
- Where does Venus appear in my chart, and how does it affect my attitude to my relationships?
- Where is Mars in my chart, and does it correctly represent my passions, drive, and sexual energy?
- Do any significant aspects appear between Venus, Mars, and other planets that influence my romantic nature?
- How does my moon sign impact my emotional needs?

## *Health and Wellness*

- What sign appears on the cusp of my 6th House, and how does it affect my attitude to health and wellness?
- How does Mars's position in my chart affect my physical energy and activity levels?
- Where does Saturn appear in my chart, and what challenges or health issues does it highlight?

- Are any aspects to my sun, moon, or 6th House planets affecting my health?

- How do transiting planets affect my 6th House, and are there any upcoming movements indicating a period for health improvements?

## *Home and Family*

- What sign appears on the cusp of my 4th House, and how does it represent my relationship to home and family?

- What planets in my 4th House are influencing my family life and emotional wellness?

- Does the moon in my chart reflect my family bonds and emotional roots?

- Will any current or upcoming transits affect my 4th House through changes in my household or family?

- How do eclipses or other transits impact my 4th House?

## *Finance and Resources*

- What sign appears on the cusp of my 2nd House, and what is its influence on my finances and security?

- Where does Venus appear in my chart, and what effect will it have on my material security?

- Where might Jupiter bring financial growth, expansion, and abundance?

- Are there any challenging aspects to my 2nd House ruler or Venus in terms of my finances?

- How do transiting planets affect my 2nd House, and when are the best times to make financial decisions?

## *Personal Growth and Spirituality*

- Where is Neptune in my chart, and what is its influence on my spirituality, intuition, and creativity?
- What sign appears on the cusp of my 9th House, and what is its influence on my attitude to higher learning, philosophy, and spiritual growth?
- Where does Pluto appear in my chart, and how does it reflect transformative experiences?
- How do major transits or progressions affect my 9th or 12th Houses and my spirituality and personal breakthroughs?
- How are eclipses or planetary transits impacting me spiritually or my opportunities for development?

## *Manifestation and Goal Setting*

- What sign appears on the cusp of my 11th House, and how does it influence my dreams, goals, and connection to social groups?
- Where does Jupiter appear in my chart, and how can my goals and abundance benefit from it?
- What transits or progressions are influencing my 11th House, and how can I use them to for my future goals?
- Which harmonious aspects to my midheaven, sun, or Jupiter support me in achieving my goals?

- How can I take advantage of upcoming new or full moons to set my intentions and manifest the changes aligned with my birth chart?

## Your Birth Chart

Compiling your own chart will help you to learn the basics as you get familiar with astrology. There are available online options where you can enter your details and the site will generate a chart for you. I have found that some of the generated information they provide is still pretty general and may not quite resonate. Being computer generated, they possibly lack the ability to combine certain features in the chart and there is no intuitive guidance.

These are, however, great to use as a reference that you can see and work with alongside the information and explanations provided throughout the previous chapters. In fact, I highly recommend you download your birth chart.

You'll need certain details when generating your birth chart. Here's a simple guide on how to do it.

1. Gather your birth information.

    a. **Your birth date:** The exact date of birth including date, month, and year. This will determine the celestial movement at the time and give some perspective of what planetary influences were present.

    b. **Your time of birth**: Be as accurate with this as possible, and I mean down to the minute. If you don't know, ask your family if they remember whether it was in the morning, afternoon, or night. For example, a client knew that she was born between 7am and 12pm. She could determine this because her mother had said that her father had left for work at 7am and by the time he took his lunch at midday, she had been born.

Information like this, while not 100% accurate, still helps a great deal.

c. **Location:** The town or city and country of your birth are important too. The latitude and longitude can narrow down the degrees of planets and how these affect you.

2. Choose an online birth chart calculator such as *Astro-Seek, Astro.com, Cafe Astrology, Astro Charts*, and *Astrology.com*

3. Enter and submit your birth information: Some sites will also ask for your name or gender, although this has got nothing to do with the chart and is usually for their system demographics.

4. Your chart will be generated.

Your generated chart is usually emailed to you and will reflect details that you will require as you make your way through the following chapters.

Your birth chart will tell you:

- Your star sign which represents your character (who you are) and your ego.

- Your ascending, or rising sign, represents your public personality and how the world sees you.

- Your moon sign represents your inner self such as your emotions, feelings, and intuition.

- Where the planets were as well as the star sign and house they appeared in. Planetary characteristics show up in the areas of your life that they govern or influence.

- The houses represent various areas of your life, and the planets that appear in them influence the way these areas unfold.

- Aspects indicate the angles between planets and how these interact and influence each other.

- Transits are celestial movements and subtly affect events in your life.

## Personal Astrology Basics

There are some basics that are good to have on-hand that are useful as you ask questions and that you can refer back to. Keep a journal to track your charts, the questions you answered, and the likely outcome. These will help you track your accuracy in reading charts.

### *Your Personal Plan: Step-By-Step*

1. Always have your birth chart on-hand. You'll need it for every other type of chart.

2. Study the characteristics of the 12 zodiac signs (Chapters 1 and 2). Each plays a part in your life and will appear somewhere in your chart.

3. Learn about the celestial bodies including the planets, asteroids, and nodes (Chapters 3 and 4). They are each associated with different zodiac signs and have certain characteristics.

4. Understand what each of the 12 houses represent and how they are affected by the celestial bodies occupying them (Chapter 3).

5. The aspects (Chapter 4) determine the interact of planets and are divided into various types of angles.

6. Get familiar with your ascendant sign (Chapter 2), as it is an important facet of your personality. It is always in the first house and determines where the rest of the placements in your chart fall.

7. Define your key placements which consist of your sun, moon, and rising sign.

8. Examine the key placements of the planets in each of the 12 houses to gain insights into your career (10th House), relationships (7th House), finance (2nd House), and home (4th House).

9. Identify your strong points and areas that need development. These can be pointed out by the aspects and trines in your chart.

10. Track current and future transits (Chapter 6), as these can be used for predictive purposes. Start with Saturn and Jupiter transits which indicate major periods of growth or change.

11. Identify where you can gain the most benefit and growth through aligning with celestial influences. Align your goals with the planets, houses, and aspects to get the most out of them.

By following these steps, you'll have a clearer understanding of your personal astrology and how to use it for self-awareness and planning.

## *Personal Action Plan*

To create a personal action plan, you'll follow the similar steps as with your personal plan.

1. Generate your birth chart.

2. Check current planetary placements, including houses and zodiac signs.

3. Identify major aspects to see how these are influencing your life and where you should work on personal growth.

4. Check current transits and how they affect your chart. The timing of these is important for making decisions.

5. Set your goals by aligning with anticipated influences.
6. Use your journal to record emotions and events at the time and to check back to see how your goals were supported.

## Additional Charts

The steps for any chart are simple once you know how. While they are varied, the basics remain the same with just a few minor changes for each, depending on what and why you're using a particular chart.

### *Transit Chart*

1. Refresh your memory about transits (Chapter 6).
2. Generate your birth chart.
3. Use your preferred website to calculate a transit chart. This could be grouped under tabs such as "extended charts" or similar.
4. Set the date and time to track transits. This could be the current date to see influences affecting you, or it could be a future date that coincides with events that affect you such as job interviews, buying a car, or moving house.
5. Identify transiting planets by looking at the middle and outer planets for long-term plans, and then the inner planets which may affect you in the short-term.
6. Identify which houses the transiting planet is in because this would be the area affected by the movement.
7. Check whether there are any significant aspects that may affect the chosen date and time.

8. Combine all the above to gain a full picture of the effects. For instance, Jupiter transiting your 7th House (partnerships) in a trine to your sun, may indicate opportunities for positive growth in relationships.

9. Make a note of the dates and effects and use them to plan events and activities.

10. Keep track of the transits so plans can be adjusted where necessary and as a referral when checking back to see the influences they had.

## *Solar Return Chart*

1. Refresh your memory on solar returns (Chapter 10).

2. Generate your birth chart.

3. Use your preferred website to calculate a solar return chart. This could be grouped under tabs such as "extended charts" or similar.

4. Populate the required fields and include your *current* location. Solar return charts are calculated based on where you are on your birthday because it affects the position of the houses.

5. Examine key features of the chart.

    a. The sun highlights the focus for the coming year.

    b. The moon indicates your emotional state for the year and your home and family.

    c. The ascendant sets the tone for the year showing how you will approach the year ahead and the way others see you.

    d. Houses with planets will reflect which areas will see the most activity.

6. Check whether there are any significant aspects.
7. Identify major transits for significant changes or events.
8. Combine all the above to gain a full picture of the effects.
9. Refer to your chart to stay connected to the year's energy and make adjustments if necessary.
10. Integrate the solar return chart with your birth and transit charts to get an overview of how the coming year will develop.
11. Keep a record of your chart, events, and emotions to refer back to.

## *Lunar Return Chart*

1. Refresh your memory on lunar returns (Chapter 10).
2. Generate your birth chart.
3. Use your preferred website to calculate a lunar return chart. This could be grouped under tabs such as "extended charts" or similar.
4. Populate the required fields and include your *current* location. Lunar return charts are calculated based on where you are as it affects the position of the houses.
5. Examine key features of the chart.
    a. The lunar return moon determines your emotional focus for the month ahead.
    b. The sun indicates the focus areas for the month.
    c. The ascendant sets the energy until the next lunar return, it determines your approach too.

d. Houses with planets will reflect which areas will see the most activity.

6. Check whether there are any significant aspects.
7. Identify major themes by noting the house the moon is in.
8. Combine all the above to gain a full picture of the effects.
9. Integrate the lunar return chart with your birth chart to see how the month's emotional experiences may align with your broader life journey.
10. Use your lunar return chart to plan for the month ahead by noting your emotional energy and focus areas.
11. Keep a record of your chart, events, and emotions to refer back to and note how your emotional and spiritual focus evolves.
12. Repeat every month.

## *Progressed Chart*

1. Refresh your memory on progressed charts (Chapter 10).
2. Generate your birth chart.
3. Use your preferred website to calculate a lunar return chart. This could be grouped under tabs such as "extended charts" or similar.
4. Set the date that you want to examine. This can be a current or future date. Remember, a progressed chart demonstrates a longer shift than a transit chart.
5. Note key components.
   a. Progressed Sun: This will give a view of your evolving identity, energy, and purpose. Changing about every 30 years, it marks major life shifts.

b. Progressed Moon: Possibly the most indicative of short-term changes, it changes signs every 2-3 years, reflecting emotional change.

c. Progressed Ascendant: This indicates change in the way you present yourself and how others perceive you.

d. Progressed Venus and Mars: These planets indicate changes in love, relationships, and actions.

e. Outer Planets: Jupiter and Saturn move slowly and play a role in the long-term.

6. Check whether there are any significant aspects.

7. See whether there are any major transits.

8. Compare the progressed chart with your birth chart to see what influences are affecting you.

9. Pay attention to the phase of the moon at the time of the progressed chart and apply what you've learned about lunar phases (Chapter 6).

10. Combine all the above to gain a full overview of how you may be affected either currently or at a future date and plan changes accordingly.

## *Synastry Chart*

1. Refresh your memory on synastry charts (Chapter 8).

2. Use your preferred website to calculate a birth chart for both you and your partner.

3. Request a synastry chart. Both sets of information will need to be submitted.

4. The site will generate two birth charts and overlay them, enabling you to see where the planets and houses are in both charts.

5. Note key components (sun, moon, ascendants) and compare them to see how you each express yourselves. Comparing these will show you where you are compatible and which areas need work.

6. Compare personal planets (Chapter 6) to get an idea of your relationship dynamics. Include Juno, the asteroid in your comparison.

7. Check whether there are any significant aspects between the two charts. These reveal influences that affect the relationship.

8. Pay attention to the 5th, 7th, and 8th Houses, as these are associated with relationship dynamics. See how they fall in each other's charts.

    a. The 7th House shows the approach to long-term relationships.

    b. The 5th House relates to sexual energy, playfulness, creativity, and intimacy.

    c. The 8th House relates to sexual energy and intimacy.

9. Consider emotional (moon, sun, Venus, Mars), communicative (Mercury), and attraction (Venus, Mars) compatibility.

10. See whether there are any significant aspects and identify which indicate challenges and those that indicate positive, supporting facets.

11. Combine all the above to gain a full overview of whether your relationship is balanced, challenging, or harmonious.

12. Keep track of how the dynamics play out.

## *Composite Chart*

1. Refresh your memory on composite charts (Chapter 8).
2. Use your preferred website to calculate a birth chart for both you and your partner.
3. Request a composite chart. Both sets of information will need to be submitted.
4. The site will generate a relationship chart.
5. Note key components.
    a. Sun: This will give an idea of the theme or purpose of a relationship.
    b. Moon: The emotional tone, hidden feelings, and nurturing approach are revealed here.
    c. Ascendant: This reveals how the relationship is presented and how others see it.
    d. Houses: The planets in the houses indicates what areas the relationship is likely to be focused on.
6. Check whether there are any significant aspects between the two charts. These show the way the couple interact.
7. Pay attention to the 4th, 5th, and 7th Houses, as these are associated with relationship dynamics. See how they fall in each other's charts.
    a. The 7th House shows how the relationship will function as a whole.
    b. The 4th House is associated with home life, family, and emotional security.

c. The 5th House relates to sexual energy, playfulness, creativity, and intimacy.

8. See whether there are any significant aspects and identify which indicate challenges and those that indicate positive, supporting facets.

9. Combine all the above to gain a full overview of the dynamics within your relationship as well as the purpose. See where it will thrive and what areas will need work. Reflect on how it will help you both grow, whether it's a romantic, business, or creative relationship.

10. Keep track of how it plays out and how you learned and grew from the experience.

## Targeted Areas Charts

Once you've mastered basic chart-making, start applying astrology to specific life areas such as career, relationships, and personal transformation.

### *Career Opportunities*

1. Generate your birth chart.

2. Focus on the key houses (3rd, 9th) and look at which signs and planets appear there including those on the cusp.

3. Identify where the associated celestial bodies are (Mercury, Jupiter, moon) and their placement in signs and houses.

4. Check the aspects between each of the relevant planets as well as other planets to see the challenging and harmonious influences they have on this area of your life.

5. Analyze the current transits to see how they interact with your birth chart, the way they currently influence you, and if they indicate opportunities.

6. Use progressions for long-term planning and changes.

7. Check whether there are any eclipses that may bring about sudden changes related to the area you're examining.

8. Track and journal your progress over time. Note your habits and tendencies now and compare them at intervals to see your growth or progress.

## *Chart for Health and Vitality*

1. Generate your birth chart.

2. Focus on the key houses (1st, 6th, 12th) and look at which signs and planets appear there including those on the cusp.

3. Identify where the associated celestial bodies are (sun, Mars, Saturn, moon) and their placement in signs and houses.

4. Check the aspects between each of the relevant planets as well as other planets to see the challenging and harmonious influences they have on this area of your life.

5. Analyze the current transits to see how they interact with your birth chart, the way they currently influence you, and what they indicate in terms of physical and emotional health and wellness.

6. Consider planets in retrograde, as they can affect our energy levels and mental clarity. Use them as a time to rest and evaluate our health habits.

7. Create a wellness plane unique to your health needs including consumption, exercise, and spiritual practices such as meditation. Remember, Aries is suited to high impact exercise, while a Libra may prefer yoga.

8. Refer to your solar return chart for clues about your health for the coming year. Keeping an eye on progressions can also indicate where you should pay attention to your health.

9. Check whether there are any eclipses that may bring about sudden changes related to the area you're examining.

10. Track and journal your progress over time. Note your habits and tendencies now and compare them at intervals to see your growth or progress.

## *Chart to Make Decisions*

1. Generate your birth chart.

2. List the questions related to the decision you want to make. Be specific.

3. Identify the key houses and look at which signs and planets appear there.

4. Identify where the associated celestial bodies are (sun, Mars, Saturn, moon) and their placement in signs and houses.

5. Check the aspects between each of the relevant planets as well as other planets to see the challenging and harmonious influences they have on this area of your life.

6. Analyze the current transits to see how they interact with your birth chart and the way they currently influence the area you need to make a decision on.

7. Note any major transits, returns, or retrogrades, as these will affect your decision.

8. Use progressions to your benefit—remember, we've mentioned timing—so set timelines for your decisions.

9. Track and journal your progress over time. Note your question, decision, and the outcomes based on implementing astrology when making them.

## *Chart for Home and Family*

1. Generate your birth chart.

2. Focus on the key houses (2nd, 4th, Imum Coeli, 8th) and look at which signs and planets appear there including those on the cusp.

3. Notice the sign and house placement of your moon which indicates your emotional relationship with your home environment.

4. Identify where the associated celestial bodies are (Venus, Saturn Jupiter) and their placement in signs and houses.

5. Check the aspects to the moon and 4th House as well as other planets to see the challenging and harmonious influences they have on this area of your life.

6. Analyze the current transits to see how they interact with your birth chart, the way they currently influence you, and if they indicate changes to home and family.

7. Use progressions for significant or long-term and changes. A progressed moon moving through your 4th House may coincide with moving homes, family growth, or a change in the way you relate to family members.

8. Check whether there are any eclipses that may bring about sudden changes related to the area you're examining.

9. Track and journal any changes in this area.

## *Chart for Communication and Learning*

1. Generate your birth chart.
2. Focus on the key houses (3rd, 9th) and look at which signs and planets appear there including those on the cusp.
3. Identify where the associated celestial bodies are (Mercury, Jupiter, moon) and their placement in signs and houses.
4. Check the aspects between each of the relevant planets as well as other planets to see the challenging and harmonious influences they have on this area of your life.
5. Analyze the current transits to see how they interact with your birth chart, the way they currently influence you, and if they indicate opportunities.
6. Use progressions for long-term planning and financial changes.
7. Check whether there are any eclipses that may bring about sudden changes related to the area you're examining.
8. Track and journal your manifesting progress over time.

## *Chart for Stress Relief and Wellness*

1. Generate your birth chart.
2. Focus on the key houses (1st, 6th, 12th) and look at which signs and planets appear there including those on the cusp.
3. Identify where the associated celestial bodies are (Mars, moon, Saturn, Neptune) and their placement in signs and houses.
4. Analyze the current transits to see how they interact with your birth chart and the way they currently influence your current stress and wellness cycles.

5. Use progressions for long-term health and wellness planning.
6. Check whether there are any eclipses that may bring about sudden changes in your physical and mental health.
7. Create a routine aligned with your chart in terms of stress and wellness.
8. Track and journal how the astrological movements and influences affected your health.

## *Personal Transformation: Outer*

1. Generate your birth chart.
2. Identify key themes to help you understand your character as a whole.
    a. Sun, moon, and ascendant: Understand each and how they relate to you.
    b. Identify dominant elements: Do you have a balance, or are there more elements of one type than others?
    c. Look at planetary clusters: Are there clusters? Which houses are they in?
3. Focus on the key houses (1st, 2nd, 5th, 10th) and look at which signs and planets appear there including those on the cusp.
4. Identify where the associated celestial bodies are (Jupiter, Saturn, Mars, Venus) and their placement in signs and houses.
5. Check the aspects between each of the relevant planets as well as other planets to see the challenging and harmonious influences they have on this area of your life.
6. Analyze the current transits to see how they interact with your birth chart, the way they currently influence you, and if they indicate opportunities.

7. Use progressions for planning and making changes.
8. Set your goals and aspirations.
9. Draw up action plans and set timelines.
10. Track and journal your progress over time adjusting plans as transits evolve.

## *Personal Transformation: Inner*

1. Generate your birth chart.
2. Focus on the key houses (4th, 8th, 9th, 12th) and look at the signs and planets in the houses including signs appearing on the cusp of the 8th House.
3. Identify where the associated celestial bodies are (Pluto, Uranus, Saturn, Neptune) and their placement in signs and houses.
4. Check the aspects between each of the relevant planets as well as other planets to see the challenging and harmonious influences they have on this area of your life.
5. Analyze the current transits and to see how they interact with your birth chart, the way they currently influence you, and if they indicate transformation. Check whether any of the transformative planets are in return.
6. Use progressions to track inner growth and changes.
7. Track and journal your progress over time.

## *Manifesting Chart*

1. Generate your birth chart.
2. Be clear with your intentions and what you want manifested and align them with those areas in your chart where you excel.
3. Focus on the key houses (2nd, 10th) and look at the sign and any planets appearing there.
4. Check the aspects between each of the relevant planets as well as other planets to see the challenging and harmonious influences they have on this area of your life.
5. Analyze the current transits to see how they interact with your birth chart, the way they currently influence you, and if they indicate opportunities.
6. Check whether there are any retrogrades in play.
7. Use progressions for long-term planning and changes.
8. Work with the lunar cycles when wanting to manifest.
9. Check whether there are any eclipses that may bring about sudden changes related to the area you're examining.
10. Create a manifestation chart aligned with your chart using visualization, crystals, and affirmations.
11. Track and journal your progress over time. Include your manifestations and planetary cycles.

## *Chart for Manifesting Success, Wealth, and Abundance*

1. Generate your birth chart.

2. Focus on the key houses (2nd, 8th, 10th, 11th) and look at which signs and planets appear there including those on the cusp.

3. Identify where the associated celestial bodies are (Venus, Jupiter, Saturn) and their placement in signs and houses.

4. Check the aspects between each of the relevant planets as well as other planets to see the challenging and harmonious influences they have on this area of your life.

5. Analyze the current transits to see how they interact with your birth chart, the way they currently influence you, and if they indicate opportunities.

6. Use progressions for long-term planning and financial changes.

7. Check whether there are any eclipses that may bring about sudden changes related to the area you're examining.

8. Create a manifestation plan that's aligned with your birth chart focusing key dates.

9. Track and journal your manifesting progress over time.

## *Manifesting Ritual to Use With Your Chart*

1. Set your intention. Be clear in your intention with detailed goals or desires.

2. Align your intention with celestial movements and refer to your birth chart to see which houses and planets are relevant to your intention and avoid manifesting during Mercury retrogrades.

3. Use the lunar cycles to your benefit.

4. Align your ritual with supportive planetary transits to enhance your manifestation.

5. Choose the planets and houses relevant to your purpose. For instance, for career goals, focus on your 10th House, midheaven, and Saturn.

6. Prepare for your ritual.

    - Choose a place where you feel comfortable; somewhere that is quiet and you won't be interrupted.

7. Include tools for your ritual.

    - Candles: Choose colors that align with your goal (green for wealth, pink for love, white for clarity).

    - Crystals: Use stones that resonate with the planetary energies like Rose Quartz for Venus or Citrine for Jupiter.

    - Astrological Symbols: Include symbols or items related to the planets or houses involved in your manifestation. For instance, to manifest love you might gather a few pink rose petals.

1. Write an affirmation aligned with your intention. For example, "I attract financial abundance into my life with ease and gratitude."

2. Visualize your desired outcome as though it's already manifested.

3. Invoke the energy of the relevant planet. Focus on and call on the relevant planet. For instance, if manifesting love, call on Venus as you light a pink candle and meditate on her qualities.

4. Take action. Working toward your goal sets your manifestation in motion.

5. Close your ritual by expressing gratitude to the universe, planets, and yourself.

6. Release your intention and trust that the universe is working in your best interests, aligning with your goals, and allow the manifestation process to unfold naturally.

## Advanced Topics

Creating astrological forecasts involves tracking transits, moon phases, eclipses, retrogrades, and progressions and interpreting how these cosmic events affect your natal chart.

### *Forecasting*

1. Generate your birth chart.

2. Check the aspects between each of the relevant planets as well as other planets to see the challenging and harmonious influences they have on this area of your life.

3. Track current transits. See how they compare with the planets in your birth chart.

4. Pay attention to lunar progressions to see if it has moved into a new house or sign which would indicate a change of focus.

5. Check whether there are any planets in retrograde and how these may affect outcomes.

6. Check whether there are any eclipses that may bring about sudden changes related to the area you're examining.

7. Take note of any lunar phases and work with them.

8. Observe solar and lunar returns for monthly and yearly forecasts.

9. Combine all observed movements to create a personalized timeline of upcoming influences and use them to your advantage.

10. Track and journal your forecasting progress over time.

### *Financial Growth*

1. Generate your birth chart.

2. Focus on the key houses (2nd, 8th, 11th) and look at which signs and planets appear there including those on the cusp.

3. Identify where the associated celestial bodies are (Venus, Jupiter, Saturn, Pluto) and their placement in signs and houses.

4. Check the aspects between each of the relevant planets as well as other planets to see the challenging and harmonious influences they have on this area of your life.

5. Track current transits. See how they compare with the planets in your birth chart and influence your finances.

6. Pay attention progressions for long-term financial planning.

7. Check whether there are any eclipses that may bring about sudden changes related to the area you're examining.

8. Combine all observed movements to create a timeline of upcoming influences and use them to your advantage.

9. Track and journal your forecasting progress over time.

# Conclusion

As I watched Emma leave my cozy cottage, the chilly evening air seemed to wrap around her like a comforting blanket. I felt a deep sense of satisfaction, knowing I had shared with her the wisdom of the cosmos.

"You see," I began softly, speaking to the shadows that danced in the firelight, "life is a tapestry woven from our choices, experiences, and, yes, the stars above us. When I handed Emma her cosmic compass, I wasn't just offering her guidance; I was inviting her to explore the boundless possibilities that lay before her."

Astrology, I thought, is more than charts and symbols; it's a mirror reflecting the complexity of our very being. Each celestial alignment tells a story, a narrative we can choose to embrace or resist. It teaches us that our strengths and weaknesses are part of a greater design, one that we can learn to navigate with grace. I remembered the moments we shared and the way Emma's eyes lit up as I explained the significance of her Sagittarius sun and Cancer moon. "The stars can guide you, but it is you who must walk the path," I had told her. It's a sentiment I hold dear. The universe offers us insights, but ultimately, the journey is ours to undertake.

In sharing my knowledge, I hope to empower others to find their own voices and destinies. As Emma continues her exploration of astrology, I trust she will uncover the layers of her identity and the paths that lead to fulfillment. With each session, my goal remains to help others recognize that they are the authors of their own stories.

And as I settled back into my chair, the warmth of the fire wrapping around me, I smiled, knowing that every soul who crosses my threshold carries a spark of the universe within them; ready to shine, ready to grow.

In this dance of life, we are all connected by the stars, and I, Mrs. Hilda, will always be here to help guide those seeking their way.

# About the Author

Janice has been enchanted by the night sky since childhood, a fascination that has evolved into a passion for astrology. Her book, *Astrology for Beginners*, is a testament to this lifelong intrigue, blending her extensive knowledge of the stars with practical insights. As an avid stargazer, she expertly distills complex astrological concepts into accessible guidance, empowering readers to integrate the wisdom of the cosmos into their everyday lives.

With a commitment to making astrology both approachable and engaging, her work does more than impart knowledge; it invites readers to embark on a transformative journey of self-discovery and personal growth, guided by the wisdom of the cosmos.

Janice's unique ability to demystify complex concepts makes this book an invaluable resource for anyone seeking to explore the celestial world.

Beyond her work in astrology, Janice has studied a range of healing modalities, including Pranic Healing, Theta Healing, and Reiki, where she has achieved Master-level certification. Her clairvoyant abilities and deep empathic insights further enrich her practices. These diverse skills and experiences profoundly enrich her writing, weaving a rich tapestry of knowledge and insight across her various works.

Her other books include:

- *The Comprehensive Beginners Guide to Chakras*: Easy steps for balancing chakras and healing your emotions to attract love, happiness, success and more....
- *Empowered Shadow Work:* Guided gratitude journal and workbook for healing and manifesting your dream life.
- *Self-Love Shadow Work and Workbook:* For manifesting your perfect life, personal growth, and spiritual awakening.
- *Witchcraft Spell Book:* for Wiccan, psychic, modern and green witch for beginners.

Each book is a testament to her commitment to spiritual exploration and personal empowerment.

Janice's writing style is both insightful and compassionate. She seamlessly weaves together knowledge and experience, creating a holistic reading journey that enlightens the mind while nourishing the soul.

Readers often find themselves invigorated after engaging with her work, experiencing a renewed sense of purpose and zest for life.

Embrace your spiritual journey with Janice Amber Lee: Study her writings today at *https://www.amazon.com/stores/Janice-AmberLee/author/B0CHYZGPJQ*.

Join her in promoting understanding, unity, and personal growth across our ever-evolving world.

If you enjoyed Janice's book, please consider leaving a review.

# References

Accesswire. (2024, April 18). *According to latest harris poll research, americans, especially millennials, navigate their lives by the "stars."* Abc27.com/. https://www.abc27.com/business/press-releases/accesswire/853755/according-to-latest-harris-poll-research-americans-especially-millennials-navigate-their-lives-by-the-stars/

Allard, S. (2020, August 19). *5 things to know about Vedic astrology*. Hindu American Foundation. https://www.hinduamerican.org/blog/5-things-to-know-about-vedic-astrology

Annie. (n.d.). *Midheaven.* Cafe Astrology. https://cafeastrology.com/midheaven.html

Arroyo Camacho, N., & Beringer-Tobing, B. (2024, April 29). *Your monthly lunar return functions like a cosmic "reset" button—here's how to find and use yours.* Well+Good. https://www.wellandgood.com/lunar-return-astrology/

Astopia. (2024, August 13). *Mastering the 10th House: Career Goals and Social Status in Astrology* Astopia.com. https://astopia.com/en/blog/mastering-10th-house-career-goals-social-status-astrology-c-100002

Astopia. (2024). *Astrology 8th house: Transformation, intimacy and beyond.* Astopia.com. https://astopia.com/en/blog/astrology-eighth-house-transformation-intimacy-beyond-c-100002

Astra Relationships. (n.d.). *Utilizing planetary transits in astrology for timing major life decisions - astra relationships.* AstraRelationships.com.

https://astrarelationships.com/planetary-transits-and-timing-key-decisions/

Astral Oracle. (2024, July 16). *Astrological houses and their connection to health.* Medium. https://medium.com/@astral.oracle369/astrological-houses-and-their-connection-to-health-9721aaf07472

Astro Charts. (2024). *Create your composite chart.* Astro-Charts.com. https://astro-charts.com/tools/new/composite/

Astrogifts. (2023, September 22). *How to unlock your zodiac powers.* Astrology Gifts. https://www.astrogifts.org/how-to-unlock-your-zodiac-powers/

Astrograph. (2024). *The aspects.* Astrograph.com. https://www.astrograph.com/learning-astrology/aspects.php

Astrolada. (n.d.). *The astrological ages.* Www.astrolada.com. https://www.astrolada.com/articles/astrology-techniques/the-astrological-ages.html

*Astrology survey.* (n.d.). https://theharrispoll.com/wp-content/uploads/2024/02/Astrology-Survey-February-2024.pdf

AstroPush. (2024, January 13). *The power of astrology: A tool for self-discovery.* AstroPush Blog. https://astropush.com/blog/the-power-of-astrology-a-tool-for-self-discovery

AstroTwins. (2016, March 24). *Square: Planetary aspects in astrology.* Astrostyle: Astrology and Daily, Weekly, Monthly Horoscopes by the AstroTwins. https://astrostyle.com/astrology/aspects/square/

AstroTwins. (2022a, March 30). *Relationship charts in astrology: Composite and synastry.* Astrostyle: Astrology and Daily, Weekly, Monthly

Horoscopes https://astrostyle.com/astrology/relationship-charts/

AstroTwins. (2022b, April 16). *Transiting planets in astrology, explained* . Astrostyle.com. https://astrostyle.com/astrology/transiting-planets/

AstroTwins. (2022c, May 18). *2nd house astrology: The complete guide.* Astrostyle: Astrology and Daily, Weekly, Monthly Horoscopes by the AstroTwins. https://astrostyle.com/astrology/2nd-house/

AstroTwins. (2022d, June). *The IC: The roots in your chart.* Astrostyle: Astrology and Daily, Weekly, Monthly Horoscopes by the AstroTwins. https://astrostyle.com/astrology/the-ic/

AstroTwins. (2022e, December 20). *12 houses of the horoscope: The themes & lessons of each.* Mindbodygreen. https://www.mindbodygreen.com/articles/the-12-houses-of-astrology

Astrowala. (n.d.). *What type of planetary position is the basis of medical astrology?* Astrowala. https://astrowala.com/planetary-positions-in-medical-astrology-explained/

Backlund, R. (2024, April 2). *North node meaning in astrology: Discover your destiny using your birth chart.* StyleCaster. https://stylecaster.com/lists/north-node-meaning/

Banks, V. (2021, March 23). *Nourishing your moon sign: The path to your authentic self.* The Truth Beauty Company. https://thetruthbeautycompany.com/blogs/the-journal/nourishing-your-moon-sign-the-path-to-your-authentic-self?srsltid=AfmBOopjsyGtS_hXZnp3bbC8lfOxYq4u0orEAEZLYdiHriatl61NKMXU

Becker, A. (2019, February 8). *How your venus sign influences your love life.* Well+Good. https://www.wellandgood.com/venus-sign/

Blaquier, M. (2020, August 28). *Draconic astrology: Getting in touch with our deeper self.* Academia Astrologia Avanzada MB. https://mariablaquier.com/draconic-astrology/?v=959848ca10cc

Blaquier, M. (2021, January 6). *Draconic astrology - getting in touch with our deeper self.* Astro.com. https://www.astro.com/astrology/aa_article210601_e.htm

Brennan, C. (2021, May 20). *How to read an ephemeris - the astrology podcast.* The Astrology Podcast. https://theastrologypodcast.com/2021/05/20/how-to-read-an-ephemeris/

Britannica. (2023). Chinese zodiac explained. In *britannica.com.* https://www.britannica.com/video/238255/discover-myth-behind-Chinese-zodiac

Brown, M. (2024a, February 11). *What is astrology. A beginner's guide to the language of the sky.* InStyle. https://www.instyle.com/lifestyle/astrology/what-is-astrology

Brown, M. (2024b, September 24). *What your solar return means — and how to make the most of it.* Shape. https://www.shape.com/lifestyle/mind-and-body/astrology/solar-return-chart-meaning-astrology

Cafe Astrology. (2015). *The composite chart.* Cafeastrology.com. https://cafeastrology.com/compositechart.html

Campion, N. (2017, April 28). *How many people actually believe in astrology?* The Conversation. https://theconversation.com/how-many-people-actually-believe-in-astrology-71192

Chaudhari , K. (2023, June 19). *The significance of mars and venus in relationships.* AstroTalk Blog - Online Astrology Consultation with Astrologer. https://astrotalk.com/astrology-blog/the-significance-of-mars-and-venus-in-relationships-iakc/

Chimenti, A. (2023, August). *The astrological ages - a new way to view history.* Masteringthezodiac.com. https://masteringthezodiac.com/astrological-ages

Clement, S. (2002, May 31). *Transits and progressions.* Llewellyn.com. https://www.llewellyn.com/encyclopedia/article/131?srsltid=AfmBOoorW9__NLQ8OyDvSW2A1eX02VLkyE0-_oonnIjicd3q_X_XgH3H

Dawson, J. (2023, August 29). *Unlock the secrets of the draconic zodiac: Your spiritual guide to the soul's journey.* Good Vibe Astrology - Good Vibe Astrology: Navigating Life's Journey with the Stars as Your Guide. https://goodvibeastrology.com/unlock-the-secrets-of-the-draconic-zodiac-your-spiritual-guide-to-the-souls-journey/

Dr Louisa McKenzie. (2024, June 17). *Stars in their eyes—celebrity astrologers past and present.* The Times. https://www.thetimes.com/life-style/luxury/article/celebrity-astrologers-past-and-present-times-luxury-w5h286jcp

Early Astronomy in the University of Michigan Collections. (n.d.). *Mesopotamian constellations and their legacy.* Early-Astronomy.classics.lsa.umich.edu. https://early-astronomy.classics.lsa.umich.edu/ancient_ziqpu.php#

Farrar, A. (2022, January 6). *Why is astrology making a twenty-first-century comeback?* Www.panmacmillan.com. https://www.panmacmillan.com/blogs/lifestyle-wellbeing/the-popularity-of-astrology

Garis, M. G., & Beringer-Tobing, B. (2024, July 9). *Use your 6th house placement in astrology to maximize your daily rituals and well-being.* Well+Good. https://www.wellandgood.com/6th-house-in-astrology/

Garis, M. G., & Carefoot, H. (2022, June 1). Is your astrological opposite your best match? Here's an astrologer's take on your compatibility. *Well+Good.* https://www.wellandgood.com/opposite-zodiac-signs/

Gautam. (2023, December 28). *Cosmic conversations: Exploring the influence of planets on communication styles.* Medium. https://medium.com/@astrotaarez9/cosmic-conversations-exploring-the-influence-of-planets-on-communication-styles-db08aba22dad

Gautam. (2024, September 11). *The power of the astrological planets in your personal and spiritual growth.* Medium. https://medium.com/@astrotaarez9/the-power-of-the-astrological-planets-in-your-personal-and-spiritual-growth-7fa15077f26e

George, D. (2019, January 5). *The first five steps in learning traditional astrology.* Rubedo Press. https://rubedo.press/propaganda/2018/12/21/first-five-steps

Gill, N. (2023, April 5). *The latin names for days of the week.* ThoughtCo. https://www.thoughtco.com/latin-names-for-the-days-121024

Gillett, R. (2011). *The secret language of astrology : The illustrated key to unlocking the secrets of the stars* (pp. 61–131). Watkins.

Goddess Retreats. (2023, September 11). *A roadmap to self-care based on your moon sign.* Goddess Retreats -. https://www.goddessretreats.com/a-roadmap-to-self-care-based-on-your-moon-sign/

Gray, R. (2023, October 24). *12 zodiac signs: Dates and personality traits of each star sign.* Whatever Your Dose. https://whateveryourdose.com/zodiac-signs/

HeloAstro. (2023, November 1). *Planetary days & hours in astrology.* HéloAstro. https://www.heloastro.com/blog/planetary-days-and-hours-in-astrology

Hermes Astrology. (2024, April 9). *Jupiter in vedic astrology.* Medium.com. https://medium.com/@HermesAstrology/jupiter-in-vedic-astrology-c4e412e06c5b

Hickox, J. (2019, September 24). *The galactic center.* Living Astrology with Janet Hickox. https://living-astrology.com/the-galactic-center/

Horvat, K. (2019, July 12). *Written in the stars: Why astrology is more than a fad.* Study Breaks. https://studybreaks.com/thoughts/astrology-generation-z-millennials/

Howard, A. (2023, May 14). *What is the galactic center astrology?* Https://Elemental-Astrology.com. https://elemental-astrology.com/what-is-the-galactic-center-astrology/

Jeffery, A. (2023, January 9). *How millenials & gen Z made astrology a billion-dollar industry.* Harper's Bazaar Australia. https://harpersbazaar.com.au/why-are-people-obsessed-with-astrology/

Jenkins, R. (2018, November 27). *More than half of Britons don't know what their blood type is, survey claims.* The Independent. https://www.independent.co.uk/life-style/blood-type-positive-negative-health-weight-body-knowledge-study-a8653921.html

Jyoti. (2023, August 8). *Astrology's role in self-discovery and personal growth.* AstroTalk Blog - Online Astrology Consultation with

Astrologer. https://astrotalk.com/astrology-blog/astrologys-role-in-self-discovery-and-personal-growth-insideastro-iajj8-8/

Kelly, A. (2021, July 4). *Birth charts 101: Understanding the planets and their meanings.* Allure. https://www.allure.com/story/astrology-birth-chart-reading

Lapidos, R. (2018, July 5). *The best way to de-stress, according to your astrological sign.* Well+Good. https://www.wellandgood.com/astrology-stress-relief-for-your-sign/

Larkin, B. (n.d.-a). *Chiron in astrology: Revealing your path to healing & growth.* Tiny Rituals. https://tinyrituals.co/blogs/tiny-rituals/chiron-astrology?srsltid=AfmBOorGuiEfj1B4KT1PdK4jJ1xUAUiSejWKn8UuGaA7C8rJ7s404GFo

Larkin, B. (n.d.-b). *The 7th house of astrology: Partnerships, agreements, & relationships.* Tiny Rituals. https://tinyrituals.co/blogs/tiny-rituals/7th-house-astrology

Lee, C. (2022, July 13). *What's your type and why does it matter?* Baton Rouge General. https://www.brgeneral.org/news-blog/2022/july/whats-your-type-and-why-does-it-matter-/

Levine, M. (2020, December 10). *Lilith: The real story.* Aish.com. https://aish.com/lilith-the-real-story/

Manzella, S. (2023, November 25). *Yes, you can use astrology to choose lucky dates and times for important events—here's how.* Well+Good; Well+Good. https://www.wellandgood.com/electional-astrology/

March, M. D., & McEvers, J. (1981). *The only way to...learn astrology, volume 1* (pp. 12–20). ACS Publications. (Original work published 1976)

Maree, J. (2024, September 14). *What your "opposite zodiac sign" means in astrology.* Yoga Journal; Yoga Journal. https://www.yogajournal.com/lifestyle/astrology/opposite-zodiac-sign/

Miller, S. (2023, August 28). *Third House.* Susan Miller Astrology Zone. https://www.astrologyzone.com/learn-astrology/the-12-sectors/third-house/

Mishra, R. (2024, August 23). *How to use astrology for personal growth and self-improvement?* Medium. https://medium.com/@raveenasethi2024/how-to-use-astrology-for-personal-growth-and-self-improvement-42213913baf8

mizChartreuse. (2021, August 13). *What is a yod in astrology? What the finger of god means in a birth chart* . Astrostyle: Astrology and Daily, Weekly, Monthly Horoscopes by the AstroTwins. https://astrostyle.com/astrology/yod-in-astrology/

Montufar, N. (2024, September 1). *12 zodiac signs: Dates, symbols, facts, & personality traits for each.* Www.astrology.com. https://www.astrology.com/zodiac-signs

Moon Omens. (2023, September 27). *The astrological ages: A spiral of time.* Moon Omens. https://www.moonomens.com/the-astrological-ages/

Morgan. (2019, May 10). *How to read an ephemeris? Understanding the chart.* AskAstrology. https://askastrology.com/life/how-to-read-an-ephemeris/

Mukerji, T. (2022, December 21). *How mars affects a couple's sexual, emotional, and intellectual compatibility.* Hindustan Times. https://www.hindustantimes.com/astrology/horoscope/how-mars-affects-a-couple-s-sexual-emotional-and-intellectual-compatibility-101671622128839.html

Noor, S. (2023, November 22). *Gen Z's obsession with astrology is a search for something deeper.* WIRED Middle East. https://wired.me/culture/understanding-the-gen-z-obsession-with-astrology/

Otero, A., Rosenbohm, R., & Bolen, A. (2022, June 2). *Your saturn sign: What your saturn placement means astrologically.* VICE. https://www.vice.com/en/article/what-does-saturn-in-the-signs-mean-in-my-birth-chart/

Patricia Lantz C.Ht. (2022, June 15). *North node in libra: A diplomatic and individual soul.* LoveToKnow. https://www.lovetoknow.com/life/astrology/north-node-libra-diplomatic-individual-soul

Peacock, K. (2023, September 13). *This Is Your Most Powerful Chakra, Based On Your Zodiac Sign.* Collective World. https://collective.world/this-is-your-most-powerful-chakra-based-on-your-zodiac-sign/

Peterson, T. (2023, September 2). *Understanding the void of course moon: Astrological implications and activities to avoid.* Medium. https://medium.com/@ZodiacJourney/understanding-the-void-of-course-moon-astrological-implications-and-activities-to-avoid-98b953eb5ec7

Pham, T. (2018, August 20). *Planets and houses to look for in astrology when it comes to romantic compatibility.* Medium. https://medium.com/@thympham77/planets-and-houses-to-look-for-in-astrology-when-it-comes-to-romantic-compatibility-ebadcb73819f

Prokerala. (n.d.). *Solar return chart.* Prokerala.com. https://www.prokerala.com/astrology/solar-return-chart/

Pyne, S. (2023, November 1). *A complete guide to using planetary hours for manifestation?* Hindustan Times.

https://www.hindustantimes.com/astrology/horoscope/a-complete-guide-to-using-planetary-hours-for-manifestation-101698835557792.html

Pyne, S. (2024, July 9). *What is Lilith sign, and how does it impact your zodiac sign?* Hindustan Times. https://www.hindustantimes.com/astrology/horoscope/what-is-lilith-sign-and-how-does-it-impact-your-zodiac-sign-101709645611858.html

Regan, S. (2022, January 5). *Is there A grand trine in your birth chart? How to tell & what it means.* Mindbodygreen.com. https://www.mindbodygreen.com/articles/grand-trine

Reiss, A. (2023, August 4). *The most important astrology transits | california psychics.* California Psychics. https://www.californiapsychics.com/blog/astrology-numerology/most-important-astrology-transits.html

Rose, M. (2024, April 15). *Discover your ultimate stroke of luck with this one astrology placement.* Parade Astrology: Entertainment, Recipes, Health, Life, Holidays. https://parade.com/astrology/part-of-fortune-meaning-astrology#what-the-part-of-fortune-means-in-astrology

Ruiz, V. (2022, May 11). *Planning your month with your lunar return chart.* Medium. https://medium.com/@CarriedByTheCosmos/planning-your-month-with-your-lunar-return-chart-9625d8ac43e8

Amelia S. (2023, December 17). *Mars in love: How your passionate side influences relationships.* Astro Helpers. https://www.astrohelpers.com/mars-in-love-how-your-passionate-side-influences-relationships/

Saint, M. (2024, January 31). *Jupiter's abundance thursdays: Navigating prosperity and growth.* Medium.

https://medium.com/@milverton.saint/jupiters-abundance-thursdays-navigating-prosperity-and-growth-69807652116b

Sara Zarrella Photography. (2021, June 8). *Reason, season and a lifetime-poem.* Sara Zarrella Photography. https://sarazarrella.com/2010/12/reason-season-and-a-lifetime-poem/

Sayaka, A. (2023, September 6). *In Your Feelings? Here's How to Self-Regulate Based on Your Moon and Earth Signs* . GROWN. https://grownmag.com/health/astrology/in-your-feelings-heres-how-to-self-regulate-based-on-your-moon-and-earth-signs/

SelineShenoy. (2022, January 21). *The importance of right timing for success.* The Dream Catcher. https://thedreamcatch.com/the-importance-of-right-timing-for-success/

Sharma, M. (2024a, February 2). *Ketu planet in vedic astrology: Its effects and significance.* The Times of India; Times Of India. https://timesofindia.indiatimes.com/astrology/planets-transits/ketu-planet-in-vedic-astrology-its-effects-and-significance/articleshow/107343682.cms

Sharma, M. (2024b, June 27). *Powerful chakra as per your zodiac sign.* The Times of India; Times Of India. https://timesofindia.indiatimes.com/astrology/zodiacs-astrology/powerful-chakra-as-per-your-zodiac-sign/photostory/111274663.cms?picid=111275012

Sifontes, A. (2023, November 1). *Intro to Mayan astrology 101.* Luz Media. https://luzmedia.co/mayan-astrology

Soni, A. (2024, June 13). *Which planet is responsible for wealth in astrology?* Medium. https://abhisheksoni53.medium.com/which-planet-is-responsible-for-wealth-in-astrology-by-astrologer-abhishek-soni-d80131cb9246

Stardust, L. (2024a, April 15). *A guide to stelliums and what it means for your birth chart, according to an astrologer.* People.com. https://people.com/what-is-stellium-in-birth-chart-everything-to-know-8630856

Stardust, L. (2024b, May 10). *Literally Everything You Need to Know About Understanding Nodes in Your Birth Chart.* Cosmopolitan. https://www.cosmopolitan.com/lifestyle/a30198931/north-south-node-meaning-placement-birth-chart/

Stardust, L. (2024c, May 22). *All about the 12 houses in astrology and what they mean.* Peoplemag. https://people.com/everything-to-know-about-the-12-houses-in-astrology-and-what-they-mean-8652306

Stardust, L. (2024d, July 19). *A comprehensive guide to synastry astrology, according to an astrologer.* People.com. https://people.com/synastry-astrology-guide-everything-to-know-8680542#:~=A%20synastry%20chart%20depicts%20the

Stargazer. (2024, May 29). *Find your career in astrology: Profession indicators in the natal chart.* Astrology. https://advanced-astrology.com/career-in-natal-chart

The Astro Twins. (n.d.). *The progressed chart in astrology, explained* . Astrostyle. https://astrostyle.com/astrology/progressed-chart/

Thomas, K. (2024, May 14). *Your guide to planetary aspects.* Cosmopolitan. https://www.cosmopolitan.com/lifestyle/a37341996/astrology-aspects-list/

Time Nomad. (2022, October 13). *When the moon nodes turn direct.* Time Nomad. https://timenomad.app/posts/astrology/philosophy/2022/10/13/when-the-moon-nodes-turn-direct.html

Timothy S. Y. Lam Museum of Anthropology. (n.d.). *History of Chinese new year.* Timothy S. Y. Lam Museum of Anthropology.

https://lammuseum.wfu.edu/education/teachers/chinese-new-year/history-of-chinese-new-year/

Tladi, T. (2024, January 2). *Your second house — money makes the world go round - tumi tladi - medium.* Medium. https://merakihandsbytumi.medium.com/your-second-house-money-makes-the-world-go-round-a9d2239ef340

TOI Astrology. (2023, December 11). From rig veda to present: Evolution of vedic astrology. *The Times of India.* https://timesofindia.indiatimes.com/astrology/from-rig-veda-to-present-evolution-of-vedic-astrology/articleshow/105906895.cms

TOI Astrology. (2024a, April 1). *Understanding how Venus affects love and relationships in astrology.* The Times of India. https://timesofindia.indiatimes.com/astrology/planets-transits/understanding-how-venus-affects-love-and-relationships-in-astrology/articleshow/108939119.cms

TOI Astrology. (2024b, July 11). *Story of Rahu and Ketu.* The Times of India; Times Of India. https://timesofindia.indiatimes.com/astrology/others/story-of-rahu-and-ketu/articleshow/111650701.cms

TOI Astrology. (2024c, July 11). *The spiritual significance of planetary transits.* The Times of India; Times Of India. https://timesofindia.indiatimes.com/astrology/planets-transits/the-spiritual-significance-of-planetary-transits/articleshow/111650993.cms

TrustedTeller. (n.d.). *Unlock your potential: A zodiac guide to achieving goals.* TrustedTeller. https://trustedteller.com/blog/unlock-your-potential-a-zodiac-guide-to-achieving-goals

Vaishnavi, A. (2024, April 22). *Crystals to attract love: Five most powerful stones for self-love and manifesting relationships.* Hindustan Times.

https://www.hindustantimes.com/astrology/crystals-to-attract-love-five-most-powerful-stones-for-self-love-and-relationships-101712857916023.html

Watson, P. (2018, June 26). *A history of pluto through the zodiac.* Patrick Watson. https://patrickwatsonastrology.com/a-history-of-pluto-through-the-zodiac/

Waxman, O. B. (2018, June 21). *Where do zodiac signs come from? Here's the true history behind your horoscope.* Time; Time. https://time.com/5315377/are-zodiac-signs-real-astrology-history/

Wylde Moon. (2024, October 1). *Phases of the moon and their meanings.* WYLDE MOON - Holly Willoughby's Life Advice, Fashion, Beauty and Style Tips. https://wyldemoon.co.uk/the-moon/phases-of-the-moon/

Yodha App. (2023, May 16). *Struggle with decision-making and self-expression? Read this.* Medium. https://medium.com/@yodhaapp/struggle-with-decision-making-and-self-expression-read-this-1a6c33b99a8f

## Image References

AIduck. (2024). Woman night constellation virgo 8830278 [Online Image]. In *Pixabay.* https://pixabay.com/illustrations/woman-night-constellation-virgo-8830278/

Conway, M. (2024). Gemini zodiac astrology horoscope 8817374 [Online Image]. In *Pixabay.* https://pixabay.com/illustrations/gemini-zodiac-astrology-horoscope-8817374/

Darkmoon_Art. (2023a). Ai generated capricorn star sign 8016351 [Online Image]. In *Pixabay.* https://pixabay.com/illustrations/ai-generated-capricorn-star-sign-8016351/

Darkmoon_Art. (2023b). Libra star sign astrology horoscope 8016355 [Online Image]. In *Pixabay.* https://pixabay.com/illustrations/libra-star-sign-astrology-horoscope-8016355/

DebbieEM. (2023). Taurus zodiac bull flower nature 7777654 [Online Image]. In *Pixabay.* https://pixabay.com/illustrations/taurus-zodiac-bull-flower-nature-7777654/

fszalai. (2023). Horoscope astrology zodiac aries 7763611/ [Online Image]. In *Pixabay.* https://pixabay.com/illustrations/horoscope-astrology-zodiac-aries-7763611/

George_Chernilevsky. (2021, November 21). *Download astrology, symbols, aquarius. royalty-free stock illustration image.* Pixabay.com. https://pixabay.com/illustrations/astrology-symbols-aquarius-aries-6808362/

MythologyArt. (2024). Archer sagittarius astrology moon 8756544 [Online Image]. In *Pixabay.* https://pixabay.com/illustrations/archer-sagittarius-astrology-moon-8756544/

OpenClipart-Vectors. (2017, January 31). *Download earth, geocentric, jupiter. royalty-free vector graphic.* Pixabay.com. https://pixabay.com/vectors/earth-geocentric-jupiter-mars-2026315/

Tandarabun, P. (2024). AI generated fish koi pisces 8908556 [Online Image]. In *Pixabay.* https://pixabay.com/illustrations/ai-generated-fish-koi-pisces-8908556/

Verheij , B. (2024). AI generated scorpio zodiac sign 8666956 [Online Image]. In *Pixabay*. https://pixabay.com/illustrations/ai-generated-scorpio-zodiac-sign-8666956/

Verheij, B. (2024a). AI generated aquarius zodiac sign 8659797 [Online Image]. In *Pixabay*. https://pixabay.com/illustrations/ai-generated-aquarius-zodiac-sign-8659797/

Verheij, B. (2024b). AI generated zodiac sign star signs 8659794 [Online Image]. In *Pixabay*. https://pixabay.com/illustrations/ai-generated-zodiac-sign-star-signs-8659794/

ZT_OSCAR. (2024). Horoscope astrology zodiac space 8722207 [Online Image]. In *Pixabay*. https://pixabay.com/illustrations/horoscope-astrology-zodiac-space-8722207/

Made in the USA
Las Vegas, NV
02 February 2025